STUCK UP!

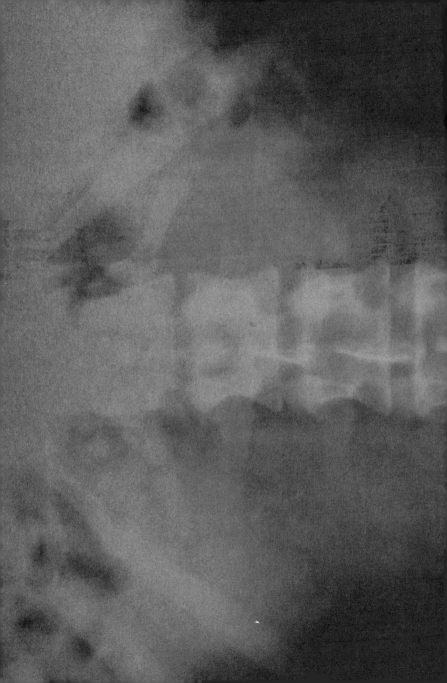

STUCK UP!

100 OBJECTS INSERTED AND INGESTED IN PLACES THEY SHOULDN'T BE

Rich E. Dreben, M.D.,

Murdoc Knight, M.D., *and*

Marty A. Sindhian, M.D.

IMAGES BY Jennifer Hale

 St. Martin's Griffin　New York

www.stmartins.com

Book design by Rich Arnold

Library of Congress Cataloging in Publication Data

Dreben, Rich E.
   Stuck up! : 100 objects inserted and ingested in places they shouldn't be /
Rich E. Dreben, M.D., Murdoc Knight, M.D., Marty A. Sindhian, M.D.
      p. cm.
   Includes bibliographical references.
   ISBN 978-0-312-68008-4 (pbk.)
   1. Wounds and injuries—surgery.   2. Penetrating wounds.
3. Ingestion.   4. Surgical emergencies.   5. Emergency medicine.
I. Knight, Murdoc.   II. Sindhian, Marty A.   III. Title.
   RD93.D74 2011
   617.1—dc23

                                                              2011026124

10   9   8   7   6   5   4

To Sujatha: Who, in the night of darkness, is the light that always guides me. To Einstein the Dog: Who has taught me more about humanity than any human being.

MARTY

To Laura Knight: Who through the years has always believed that with hard work and perseverance one day he might write a book about objects found in people's rear ends.

MURDOC

To Bossy McBossy, with love: There is no one else I would rather have boss me around, and no one else I would rather be around.

RICH

CONTENTS

ACKNOWLEDGMENTS

First and foremost, the authors want to thank their significant others, who put up with a great deal throughout this process. Each has contributed in her own special way, although, for the record, none of them served as a source for any of these images. To our patients: a HUGE thank-you for giving us the privilege to work with you and learn from you each day. We extend our heartfelt appreciation to our agent, Neil, who got stuck with us but handled everything we threw at him with much grace and expertise. We also give our profound thanks to our editor, Daniela, who diligently and patiently guided us to transform the ideas in our heads into the actual book you see before you.

We express infinite gratitude to our graphic artist, Jennifer Hale, who must be part superhero given the epic amount of work that she put into this project under strict deadlines. Thanks to her amazing talent and creativity, we are able to show our readers the kind of X-ray images doctors get to see only after both studying for years and often having a medical school debt of six figures. (In fact, with all the money we just saved you, you can definitely afford to buy a few extra copies of the book for your friends and family.) A million thank-yous and our eternal indebtedness to the anonymous eyes of all those who helped behind the scenes of *Stuck Up!,* including one pro-Pirate-Day radiologist (may your eyesight never fail) and the surgically gifted canine Sasha Wang (a big bone is on the way), among other people/dogs.

There are not enough words for Marty to adequately thank his parents, sister, brother-in-law, and nieces. It is said, "You can pick your friends but not your family." But even if he had a choice, Marty feels there is no way he could have done better. It must be his good karma that he ended up with such great people, although they may not say the same about him after they've read the book (just to be on the safe side, he is not going to ask them).

Murdoc would like to thank his parents, who, upon hearing about this book, did not say, "You went to medical school for this?" He'd also like to thank big PJ and little Andy and Alyssa, for letting him work on this book from time to time. He'd especially like to thank the little ones for not asking him what the book was about. He'll tell them in a few years.

Rich offers one final thank-you to his father, who said, "Son, I have certainly never stuck anything in my rectum." True, Dad, but you have certainly pulled many statements out of there over the years. Thanks for everything. (I know you wanted no part of this, Mom.)

PREFACE

It all started in medical school. Rich and Murdoc were close friends who partnered on everything from anatomy to basic physical exams. They were very impressed by some unique X-rays and patient stories to which they were exposed. These stories often began with patients saying something like, "I was vacuuming in the nude, when I suddenly fell and . . ." or "I was walking around the house naked, and I jumped into bed when suddenly . . ." Rich realized that the lessons he learned from these stories stuck with him more than some of the minutiae of his medical education. Because of the great learning potential inherent in these stories, Rich said to Murdoc one day, "We should remember these X-rays. I learned a ton from them," which Murdoc thought was a great idea.

Many years and X-rays later, Rich and Murdoc had still not figured out how to use this material to create an educational book that was reader-friendly and did not require the pain of going through medical school to understand it. They never quite knew when the time was right to transform their collection of memories of images and stories into something that one could proudly display on the coffee table as an instructive work. Then, during his residency, Rich met Marty, who loved the idea and provided the much-needed direction for *Stuck Up!* to become a reality.

We shared the idea with many agents and publishers, and we got some rather interesting responses (reprinting most of which is likely a violation of the majority of the fifty states' decency laws). Eventually, we found the perfect people to work with us. We quickly learned that creating the book was about as easy and straightforward as removing a coat hanger from one's rectum. (See inside the book to learn how it's done, but do not try this at home.)

For the sake of protecting patients' confidentiality while maximizing the educational value of the X-rays, we paired with an excellent graphic artist who made minor enhancements so that the objects would be more easily recognizable for our readers. On occasion we have taken creative license to add humor or flare to the situation to facilitate learning. Therefore, we present to you the standard *Law & Order*–style intro: "Although based mostly on true incidents, the following stories are technically fictional and do not depict any actual person, event, or rectum."

Often people don't know how to react when looking at these X-rays. Well, in some cases the truth is astonishing and truly hard to believe. So, our advice—just sit back, enjoy the book, and learn how to avoid doing anything that would ever end up with your end up in our next book!

—Rich, Murdoc, and Marty

INTRODUCTION

Did you know that getting objects trapped in the body is the single greatest reason for visits to the doctor? Okay, that's not really true, but it sure would make colonoscopies seem more like action films.

Truth be told, objects becoming trapped inside the body are quite common. In men, the prevalence of rectal foreign bodies is actually twenty-eight times higher than in women. As most women already know, men are always losing things!

Certainly ERs are full of people of all ages with objects inside their bodies due to various reasons. However, statistically speaking, foreign objects in the body are most likely found in someone who is either in his twenties, when one will try anything for stimulation or to relax, or in his sixties, when one will try anything just to stimulate or relax the prostate. Of course, we're not implying that men don't do stupid stuff in their thirties, forties, or fifties.

Truly, though, rectal foreign bodies are so common that they have their own section on the emedicine.medscape .com Web site. The emedicine entry mentions that controlled studies of rectal foreign bodies have yet to be done, though. Perhaps the dearth of scientific experiments regarding this practice is due to lack of volunteer enrollment?

In reality, ingested foreign bodies are overall more

common than "stuck," inserted objects. However, we have featured swallowed sundries less frequently in this book due to their perceived lower educational value for our readers. The teaching point here is that swallowed objects tend to be more common in younger children, a group with poor decision-making capacity due to factors beyond their control (unlike the fans of *The Jerry Springer Show*, who have no good excuse for their poor decision making).

No matter what you see and read here, we recommend that you do not try any of these scenarios at home, as you might end up requiring an X-ray, a surgical procedure, or face a significant risk of death or disability. For the record, we will not accept any X-rays submitted to us that were produced in an effort to re-create the vignettes and scenarios detailed in this book. So, again, please do not try this at home! Now, on the other hand, it's a different story if you just happen to have an old X-ray lying around from back when you were vacuuming in the nude or walking around naked at home when suddenly . . .

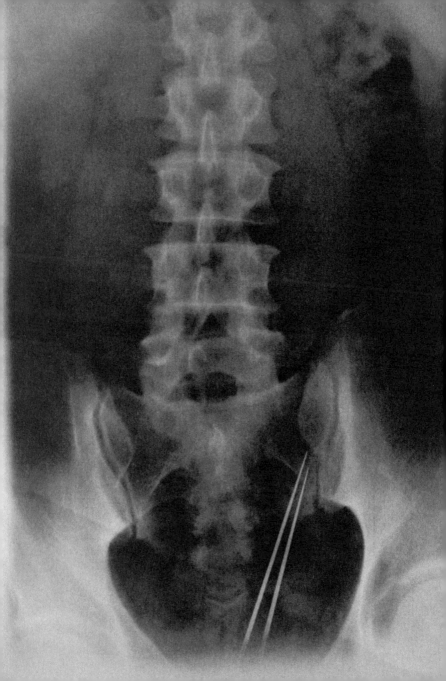

BOTTOM CHEF

Not Just for Rice Anymore

In Korean culture, some believe that one should never place chopsticks directly into a receptacle, like a bowl, in order to prop up the chopsticks. Such an act signifies death. No wonder North and South Korea always seem so stressed out.

This individual had no problem sticking his chopsticks anywhere. In fact, he may have been directly taunting death by risking an intestinal tear or infection by putting these in his receptacle.

While the chopsticks in this image are metal, chopsticks are typically made of bamboo or plastic, and, at times, bone, ivory, or wood. An August 2007 article on the *China Daily* Web site reported that the secretary general of the China Cuisine Association (CCA) said that China produced and disposed of more than 45 billion pairs of wooden chopsticks annually. The secretary general estimated that this practice cost the Chinese environment approximately 25 million trees. We're not sure what percentage of chopsticks is used for the purpose demonstrated in this X-ray, but hopefully those chopsticks are not reused afterward. That would certainly give new meaning to the word, *Pu Pu platter*.

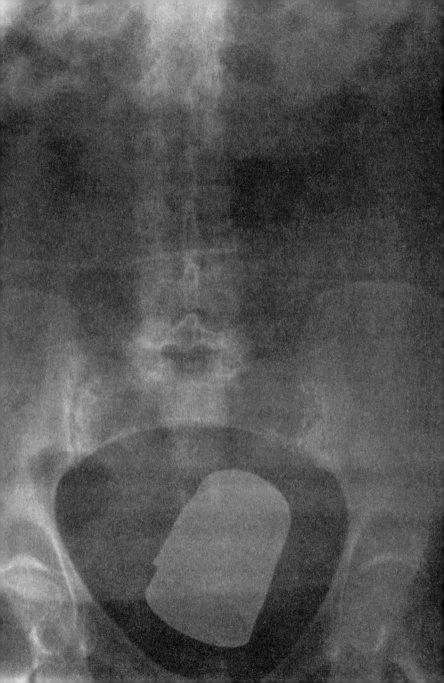

Someone Switched This Patient's
Usual Cup of Coffee with . . .

We've seen plenty of bottles stuck up patients' rears, but not nearly as many cups, even though they both hold liquids. This is not surprising given the shape of each. Images like the one in the accompanying X-ray naturally make people wonder if a cup can even get all the way up there. Doesn't the object seem much bigger than the pathway?

Basic biomechanics provide the answers here. Most skin and mucosa have certain viscoelastic properties, meaning that with enough pressure and time, one can fit surprisingly large objects through a relatively small, yet viscoelastic, space. Now you know how babies are born!

Obviously, this property is finite. There is still a limit as to how large an object can ultimately fit without causing a tear or damage. We're not sure what the record is, but we'll continue to keep track of people who try to set it.

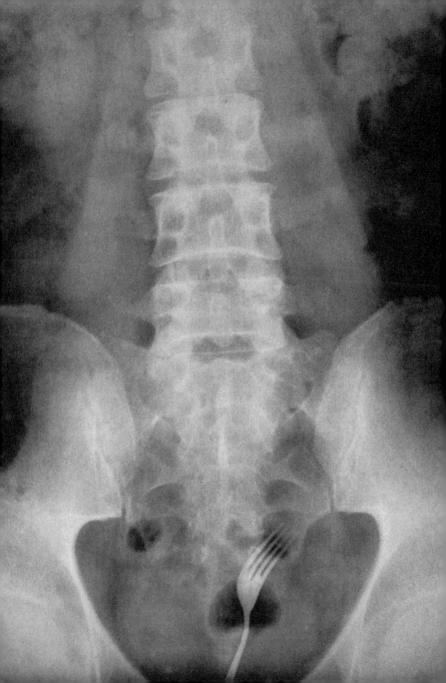

Which Fork Does Etiquette Suggest You Use Here?

For utensils to be useful for handling food, they must be long and easy to grip. This feature also makes them great for other activities, too. Often, picking the right utensil for a specific use can be a difficult task. For purposes such as this, a knife is obviously too sharp and may cause damage, while a spoon could potentially be too dull and thereby not as stimulating. Goldilocks would have probably made the same choice, assuming she did not have any mental issues after having to run for her life from three talking bears.

We think a slightly safer choice would have been a spork, although sporks are often hard to come by as they are typically used only by children, who are far too smart to do this.

The more important consideration would be the composition of the silverware. Although worse for the environment, we would hope that people choose plastic, disposable utensils for obvious reasons. Unfortunately, this patient and most others choose stainless steel, probably for the durability and easy handling. Or perhaps they finally found a reason to break out the fine china.

Ultimately, you could summarize this case by saying that when this patient reached for a fork, he took it on the road less traveled, and that made all the difference.

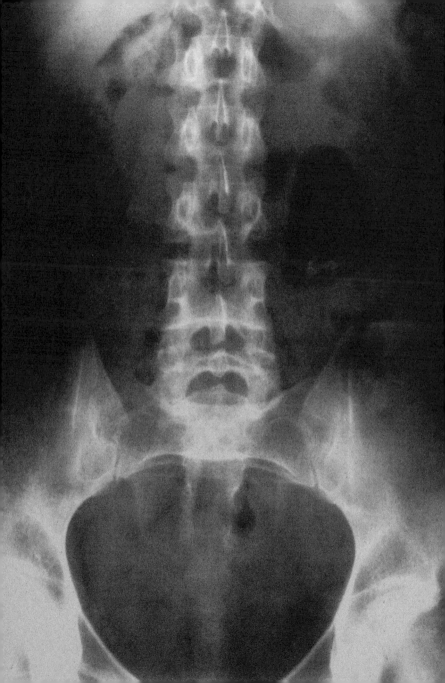

Pain in the Glass

The comedian Janeane Garofalo once quipped, "I guess I just prefer to see the dark side of things. The glass is always half empty. And cracked. And I just cut my lip on it. And chipped a tooth." Sadly, the accidental ingestion of small pieces of glass is no laughing matter.

One patient, while eating a shrimp and rigatoni dinner at his favorite restaurant, suddenly felt severe pain in his throat, followed later by chest pain. After he completed his meal—yes, *after*—the patient went to the ER, where the physician discovered glass in the patient's bowels and a perforation of the patient's esophagus. These injuries ultimately healed.

The patient asked the restaurant to reimburse him his $200 co-pay for the hospitalization, to which the restaurant agreed. We were surprised by this, considering that when we see physician procedures cause perforations, patients typically ask for far more than their co-pay. In this case, he might have at least also asked for a gift certificate for a free meal . . . at another restaurant.

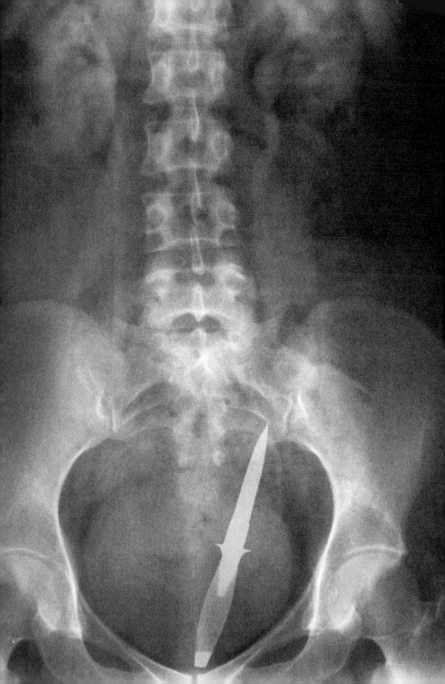

A Fishy Story

It's the same old story. A patient once explained that he spent a relaxing day fishing in the ocean. He brought his knife along to cut some bait and clean fish. He than continued the story by saying, "I was fishing, and I must have fallen asleep and rolled around on the ground where the knife was. Next thing I knew, I had this knife in me." Yet another falling asleep fishing and rolling onto a knife story. If you've heard one, you've heard them all.

What not everyone has heard of is how dangerous fish can truly be because of all sorts of special bacteria that come with fish. The bacteria can even spread to and infect the brain, which may be the true reason fish is known as brain food.

In fact, seafood comes with so many health risks that if we were to review them all it might make you the opposite of a *pescatarian,* a person who avoids eating most animals but will eat fish.

So someone might conclude from the above that if you want to win the fight against a health problem, perhaps you should have lots of cases that scare people. Maybe after this book we will actually see fewer cases of inserted or ingested foreign bodies . . . though knowing human nature, quite possibly not.

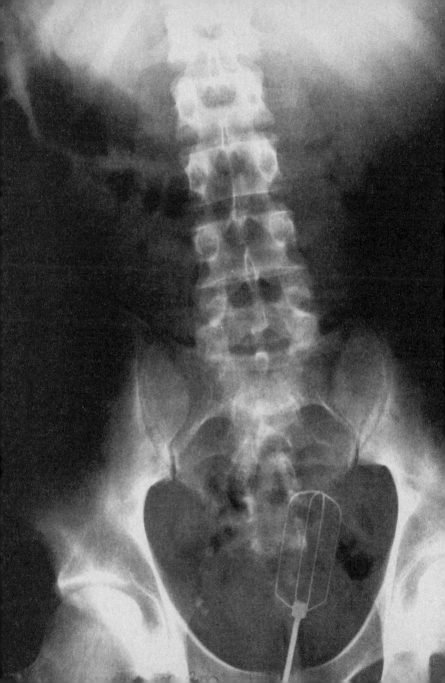

Just Beat It

This patient's reasons were obvious. Beaters work by really being able to get into and penetrate whatever they are mixing. The multiple prongs maximize what the beater can grab. With all this penetrating and grabbing, getting this beater off—*oops,* we mean, *out*—was challenging. We had to get the patient to use his sensations to direct our movements to get the beater out, as offbeat as that sounds.

Using beaters properly is particularly important when cooking a soufflé. A soufflé is composed of stiffly beaten egg whites that are folded into a sweet or savory base. You may have heard the classic lore that by opening or closing the door of the oven the soufflé may fall. This demise actually happens due to a quick change in temperature from opening and closing the door to the oven. Any grease or dirt on the cooking utensils can prevent the egg whites from rising and also lead to collapse. Therefore, upon removal, the beater in this X-ray should not be used to make a soufflé.

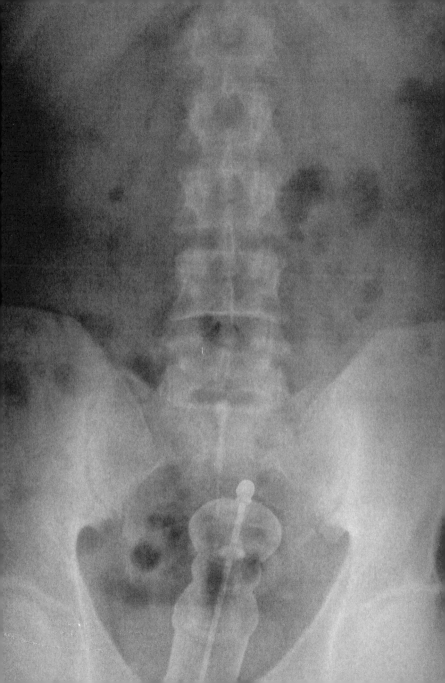

Some Sneezes May Require More Than a "Bless You"

We have peppered this vignette with all sorts of facts. Wikipedia states that black peppercorns were found stuffed in the nostrils of the Pharaoh Ramesses II, ruler of Egypt, who died more than 3,000 years ago. More recently, a pepper shaker, presumably full of ground peppercorns, was found stuffed in the rectum of this individual. This patient's medical records do not comment on whether his act was a modern interpretation of the ancient mummification ritual or whether he had heard that in ancient India, where black pepper is thought to have originated, it was used to treat conditions such as constipation, diarrhea, indigestion, cough, and nasal congestion. Using pepper to decrease nasal congestion seems as intelligent as eating spicy Indian food to decrease diarrhea.

So for those who may be tempted to follow this example, let us consider that if black pepper makes people sneeze when it's inhaled, just imagine the effect down below.

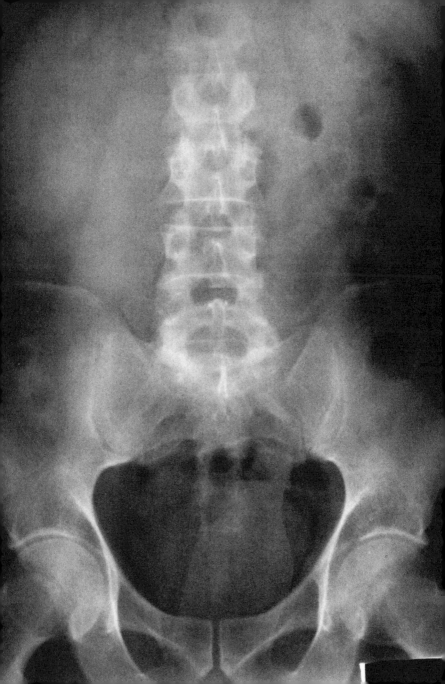

The Pepsi Challenge

This type of bottle is made of hygroscopic material, which has the ability to absorb water, like the colon. Approximately 97 out of 100 physicians recommend allowing the colon to function on its own, without the aid of a bottle. The three others replied, "No comment."

Patients who suffer from the problem of having a bottle stuck up their rear are often not honest about what happened. Here are some examples:

PATIENT A: Doc, I was vacuuming in the nude, and I fell. It was a million-to-one shot, Doc, a million-to-one.

PATIENT B: My hands were full.

PATIENT C: I swore this would never happen again. This time I made sure to put a string in the bottle and closed the cap. When I pulled the string, there was nothing on the other end.

Note the angle at which this bottle is inserted, near the prostate. An article published in *The New England Journal of Medicine* in 1985 indicated that major colas might affect sperm motility. Perhaps this patient was trying to figure this out for himself.

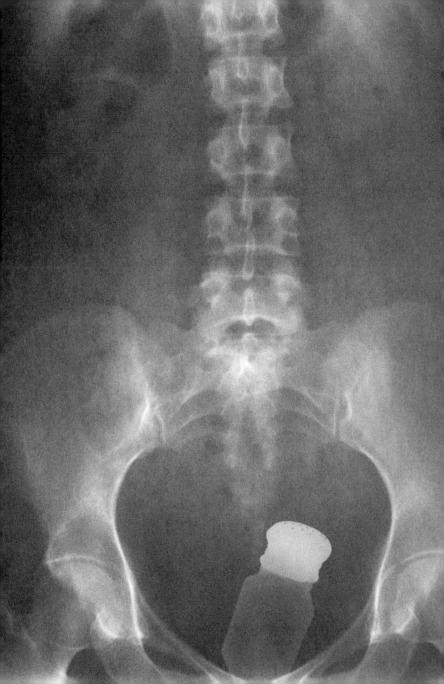

So Would It Taste Salty?

Doctors often recommend that patients reduce their daily sodium intake. One patient clearly did not heed those warnings.

Table salt is traditionally made of the compound sodium chloride. One of the most common forms of high blood pressure can be affected by salt intake. This patient had more than high blood pressure to worry about, though, which probably raised his blood pressure even more.

Salt can have some benefits. In America, salt contains iodine. If you do not have iodine, your brain sends hormonal messages to the thyroid that may cause it to grow larger and develop a goiter in an attempt to make more thyroid hormone. The thyroid gland can grow so large that it can wrap around the throat and extend down into the chest. If it could extend down a little further perhaps it could push out the salt.

If your doctor tells you to decrease your salt intake, you can remind him that use of salt in moderation can be a good thing, or you can completely ignore him. Just please don't say, "You can shove it up your butt."

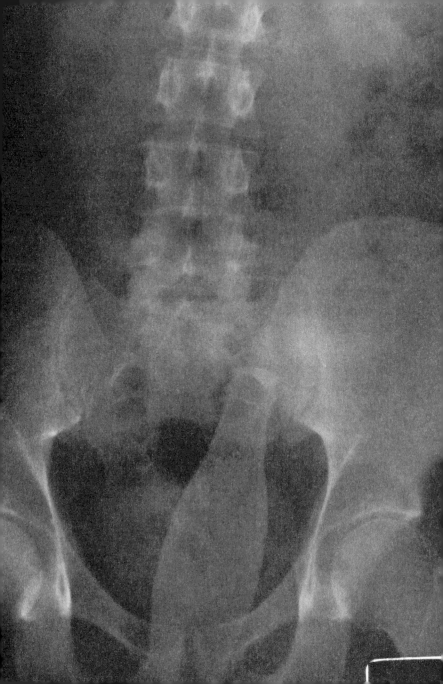

Message from a Bottle

As you have probably realized, we see a lot of bottles these days. Actually, we are seeing a lot more bottle these days. Coca-Cola's Web site states that in the 1950s, consumers first had the choice of the "traditional 6.5-ounce contour bottle" or larger bottle sizes of 10, 12, or 26 ounces of Coca-Cola in the 1980s. Today, the same product is available in 1 liter (33 ounces) and 2 liter (66 ounces) bottles. This increase in size makes the practice pictured here a little tougher.

Such an increase in portion size is not limited to Coca-Cola. A recent study examined the ratio of meal size to head size in fifty-two depictions of the Last Supper produced from AD 1000 to 2000. The results indicated that over the past millennium, main dish size has doubled.

Given these trends, the number of people who are becoming obese has also doubled. Per a recent national survey, 33.8 percent of U.S. adults are obese, meaning they have a body mass index of more than 30. The Body Mass Index (BMI) is calculated by dividing a person's weight in pounds by the square of that person's height in feet, although this system is not perfect. It does not take into consideration whether a person's weight might be comprised of muscle versus fat. Nor does it consider anything stored in the patient's bottom.

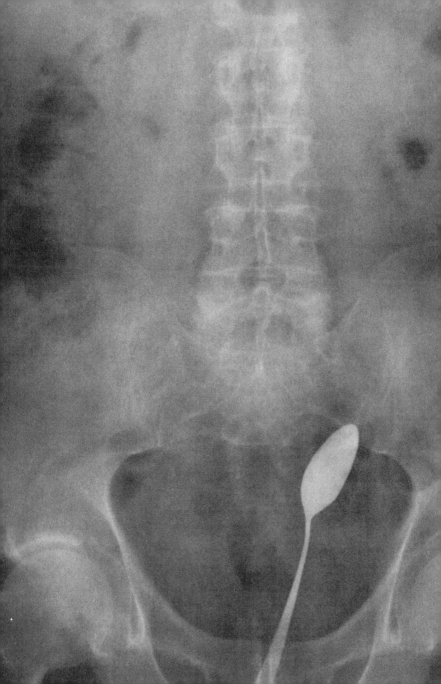

Don't Want to Be Born with This in Your Mouth

There is an old Romanian saying, "Do not put your spoon into the pot, which does not boil for you." We think there should be another saying that admonishes people not to put spoons into any opening that does not consume food for you.

In one case reported by physicians in the United Kingdom, an adult had a teaspoon removed from his colon due to the pain it caused—only ten years after he had swallowed it! Not surprisingly, this patient was drunk at the time of the ingestion, which is why you shouldn't ingest alcohol with a spoon. In 2007 an Australian woman accidentally swallowed a spoon during a laughing fit while eating pasta. In January 2010, the *Daily Mirror* reported that a bulimic woman accidentally swallowed a spoon while trying to induce vomiting. Astute readers will note the irony here. On the other hand, it can also be argued that the spoon was essentially calorie-free.

Finally, there is the case from the Netherlands that surprises even us. A female patient was found to have not one, not two, but seventy-eight different pieces of flatware in her body. That must have been quite a Pampered Chef party. At least she was smart enough to make sure none of the utensils were knives—though "smart" is probably a poor choice of words.

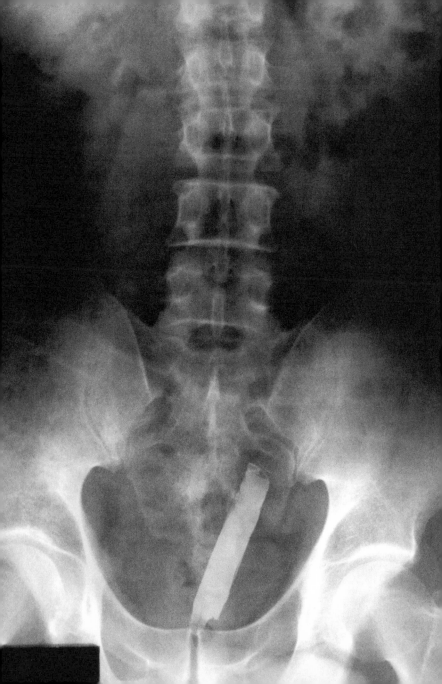

We Thought Tuna Was Good for You

Chicken of the where?

Most people we know tend to hold strong views about tuna fish, especially the smell, although the smell may not have improved with the action performed by this patient. On the one hand, some people love to eat tuna because it is high in protein and omega-3 fatty acids; others, however, are concerned about the mercury content. One thing that everybody presumably agrees on: It's the fish and not the can that you should focus on.

One patient was brought to the hospital after he reported ingesting the rolled lid of a tuna can. The patient was a prisoner with schizophrenia, so we don't know if the act was driven by the patient's possible psychotic state, or just an attempt to get out of prison. Either way it was clear the fish was no brain food for this patient.

We do know that while certain health-care providers and organizations recommend a limited amount of tuna consumption for children and pregnant women, all health-care providers recommend completely avoiding ingestion of tuna can lids.

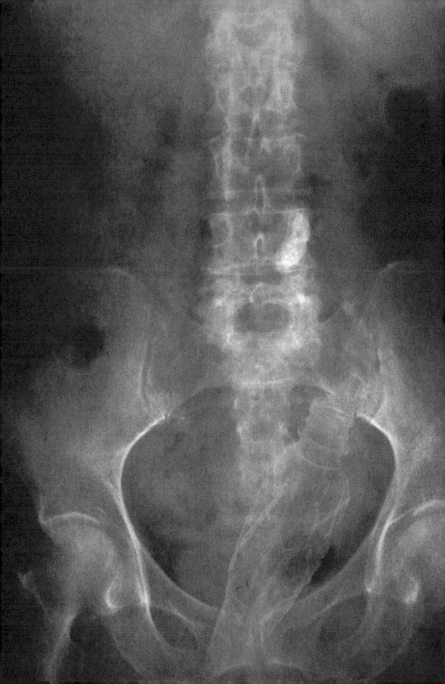

The Thirst Quencher

Our body already consists of 70 percent water, so what's the harm with a little extra? Unfortunately, this is an ineffective method of hydration. The surface of the rectum is covered by a thin layer called mucosa, which can absorb medicines rapidly. The rapid absorption enables physicians to give medications by rectum when patients cannot tolerate medications via the mouth and stomach. *Finally*, a valid reason to stick something up there.

Nevertheless, absorbing a high volume of fluid this way is impossible. The small intestine is responsible for most water absorption, while the large intestine, which is between the small intestine and rectum, actually releases water. Therefore, any fluid that's injected in the anus would cause even more fluid to come right back out, the basis of an enema and many bathroom cleanings.

Not only is this practice of water bottle insertion not beneficial, it can be harmful. Research shows that many types of plastic bottles erode and can release chemicals that are *carcinogens*, or cancer-causing substances. Some of these chemicals can have a powerful effect on our hormones and reproductive organs, and not in a male enhancement, "the time is now," little blue pill sort of way. In other words, consider forgoing the plastic bottle for a glass or stainless steel receptacle.

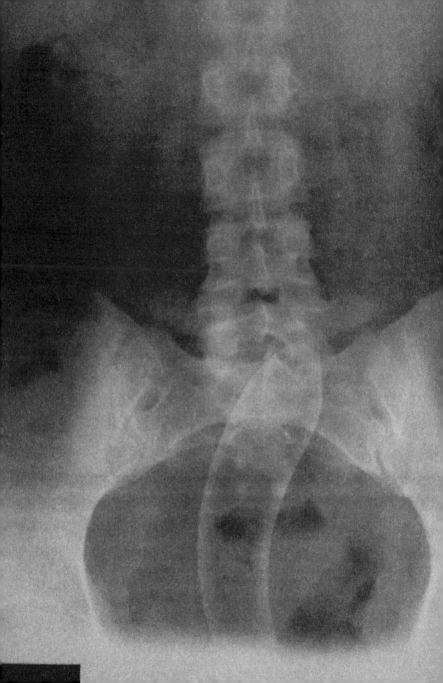

ANIMAL, VEGETABLE, OR MINERAL

Banana Boats and Banana Butts

The great wit Groucho Marx said, "Time flies like an arrow; fruit flies like a banana." According to Chiquita's Web site, bananas are the "world's most popular fruit." There is even a popular song, "Day-O (The Banana Boat Song)," dedicated to the banana workers. Here we thought beans were the musical fruit.

The fruit of the banana plant is an excellent source of potassium, vitamin B_6, vitamin C, and other nutrients, no matter what part of the gastrointestinal tract they are absorbed from. In addition to the regular use (*not* the use shown in this X-ray), other parts of the banana plant are used for a variety of purposes. Leaves are used as plates in parts of Asia; fiber from the plant is used for textiles, paper, and—surprise—banana hammocks; the sap from the plant can be used as glue. Fortunately, nothing was glued shut in this particular patient. Otherwise the high pressure may have resulted in banana pudding.

Although Chiquita's Web site is silent on where exactly the banana ranks in popularity when it comes to *this* particular usage, clinical experience suggests bananas may very well be the most popular fruit for the obvious reason of its shape. The poor pineapple never stood a chance.

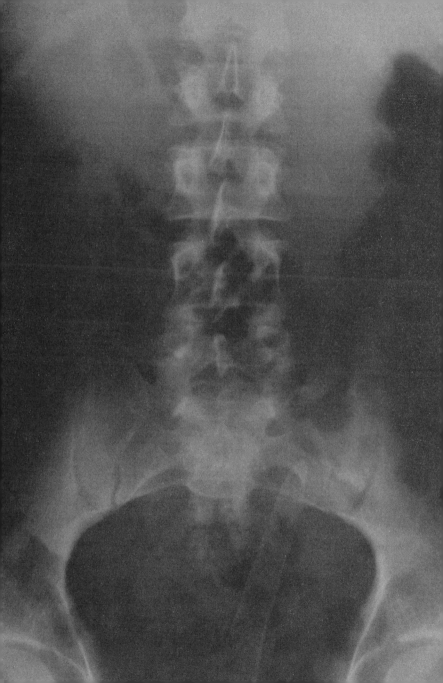

What's Up There, Doc?

The "dip" in the rectum isn't the sort of dip that was meant for carrots. Compared to many other foreign bodies, removing carrots is a piece of (carrot?) cake—as long as they are not part of a salad. Carrots can be broken into small pieces (which is how we get bite-size carrots) to facilitate their removal, and they are less likely to cause the kind of problems broken glass or a sharp metal object might cause. Plus, unlike glass or a metal object, the carrot is edible. Well, perhaps not this carrot.

Interestingly, in many cultures carrots traditionally have been used to treat constipation and other digestive complaints, which was perhaps the intention here in this patient's case. Carrots are also an excellent source of beta-carotene, which gives carrots their orange color and is converted to vitamin A in the human body. Because a lack of vitamin A can cause poor vision, many often associate carrots with good vision. Having said that, the only things you are likely to see by sticking carrots up your brown eye are the ER doctors and nurses.

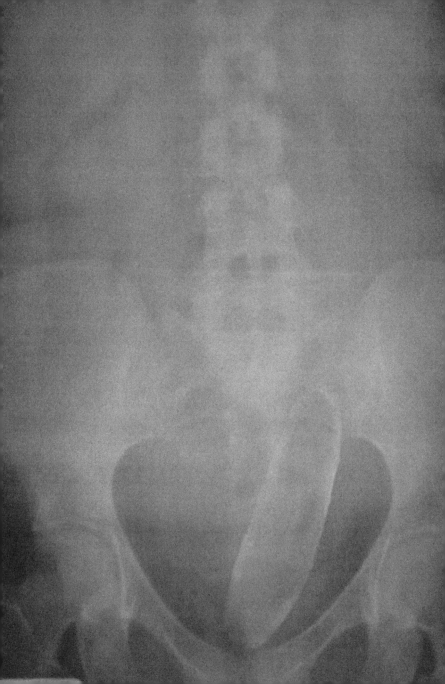

Not So Cool as a Cucumber

On *VeggieTales,* the cucumber seems so innocent, but no longer.

The Japanese ritual of suicide—called *hara-kiri*—is suicide by disembowelment. This involves stabbing oneself in the abdomen with a sword and moving it around in a slicing motion. On March 31, 2010, *The Sun* reported that a man in Hong Kong was found in a pool of blood, the cause of which was a severe rectal tear due to a cucumber up his bottom. He was taken to the hospital, where he reported that this was a suicide attempt. As far as we know this is the only case of hara-kiri with a cucumber. Jalapeño peppers on the other hand . . .

Most cases of cucumbers up the rectum or vagina are generally in the context of sexual activity, intoxication, and, of course, accidentally falling while cooking in the nude and landing on the many upright cucumbers that plague all modern kitchens. Some people admit they were just trying a new technique for pickling.

There does appear to be a certain "partnership" between the cucumber and the anus for many people. In fact, the Urban Dictionary even lists the term "anus cucumber" among its definitions and defines it as a slang term for a person who is being "silly." Hence the well-known phrase, "silly as an anus cucumber."

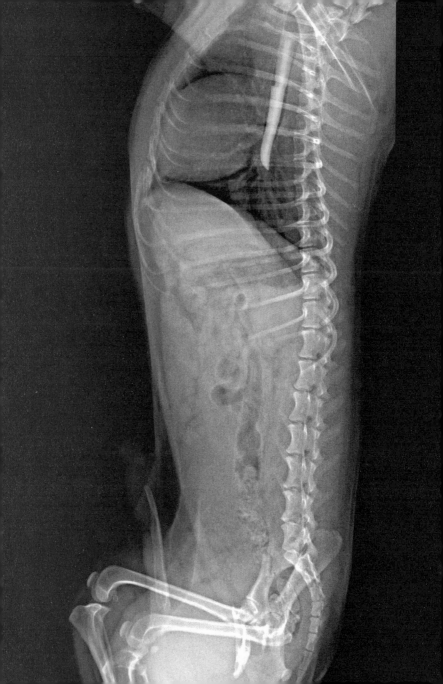

Animals Are People, Too

This case was completely an accident, as the dog was no-where near Michael Vick. It was just another holiday-related canine injury. The dog's guardian was cooking a fine holiday turkey. Next to the turkey was a knife so sharp that it was advertised as having the ability to cut through a shoe. (Reebok soufflé anyone?) Who would have thought that having such a sharp knife could come with other risks as well?

The dog remained alive but impaled. So what's the solution? Really it depends on the dog's guardian. We say this because although some people treat their pets even better than they treat themselves, others might not be willing to fork out the thousands of dollars to have the lifesaving surgery performed. Situations like this have led to the advent of pet health insurance. Such insurance enables people to help their animals should such a catastrophic, yet financially prohibitive (for many people), situation arise. We're just waiting to see a situation (and X-ray) in which one pet eats another, and the two insurances fight to see who pays.

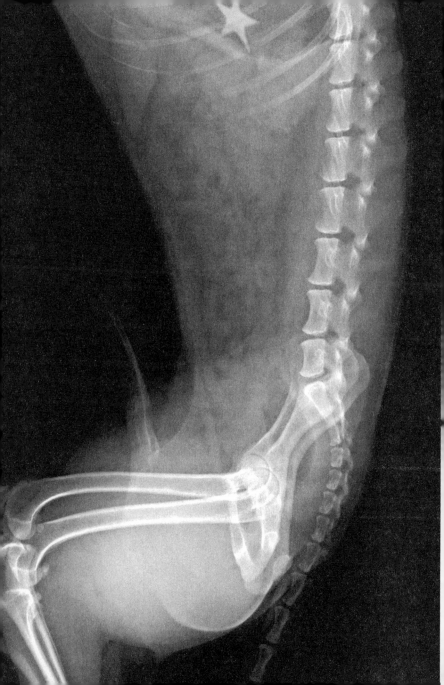

You Can Get Into the Holidays, or the Holidays Can Get Into You

We realize that after the holidays people are not always sure of what to do with their holiday decorations. We also realize that people who just want to get rid of stuff often feed it to the dog. This case was just a bad combination of the two.

Yes, this dog got into the holiday spirit by enjoying decorations and feasting all at once. Unfortunately, this was probably the worst choice of what to eat during the holiday season. The star, with all its points, makes passage both difficult and likely injurious. Fortunately, the dog was not Jewish, so he did not have to deal with the six points of the Star of David.

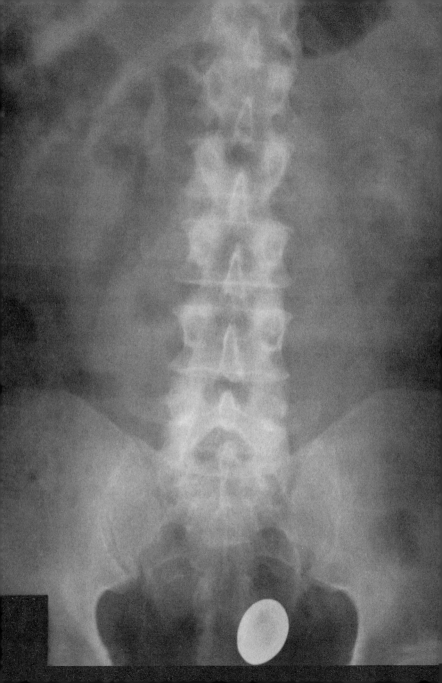

Bet You Wouldn't Have Looked Here

There's no sunny-side up with this egg. The egg in this image is only even visible because it is made of metal rather than a more lucent regular egg. If someone tried to put a real egg through such a tight area, you'd probably quickly get a scrambled egg. How chickens do it still eludes us and adds yet another layer of complexity to the "chicken-or-the-egg" mystery.

More fun with eggs can be had through chemistry. Next Valentine's Day, try to cook eggs in a tin pan. Per school chemistry lore, the heat supposedly will enable a chemical reaction to occur between the egg's sulfur, which causes the bad smell in rotten eggs, and the tin in the pan. This sulfur reaction may give off an odor that masks what might have been done with an egg before it is cooked. The result: You will end up with pink eggs. We think your partner will enjoy pink eggs on Valentine's Day, as long as you don't admit where you may have gotten the eggs.

Now, as for green eggs with or without ham, you don't want to know where those eggs have been.

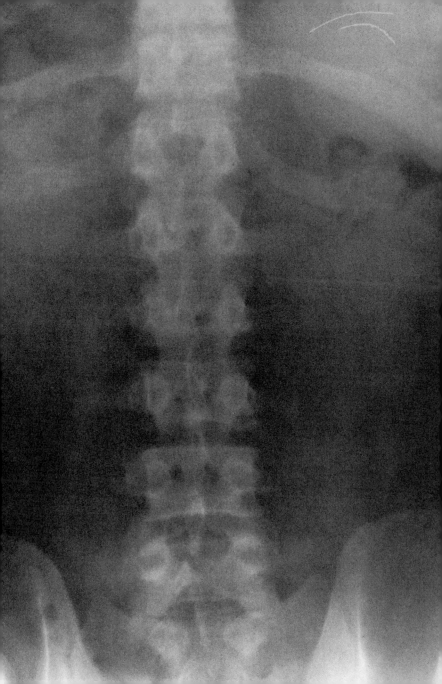

Nemo's Revenge

Despite the general perception of fish being good for one's health, this clearly isn't always the case. When surgeons do get cases like this they have to deal with jokes like: "QUESTION: *Who is the best doctor to remove fish bones?* ANSWER: *A sturgeon!*"

As sorry as we feel for the surgeons, the patients sadly fare much worse, especially the patients who present to the ER due to stomach perforations caused by swallowed fish bones. According to one study, "Fish bones are the most commonly ingested objects and the most common cause of foreign body perforation of the GI tract." After working on this book, we were starting to think it was the other stuff that we kept seeing, like multiple coins and utensils. We did not find any fish bones stuck in the rectum, but we are just waiting for someone to explain to us that he has salmon in the rear because he went swimming upstream.

In the aforementioned study, more than half of the patients experienced perforations due to swallowing fish bones. Out of fear of having such a bone-related catastrophe, many prefer to stick to eating the "healthier" alternative—hamburger—since the burger's only potential risk's involve choking, high cholesterol, and E. coli and salmonella infections.

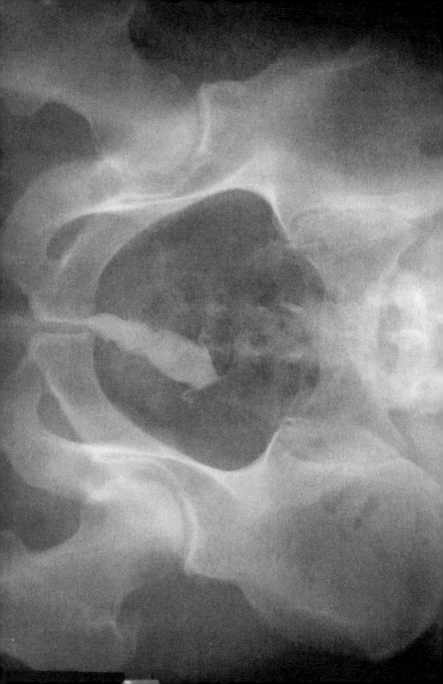

We Never Saw This on Tom and Jerry

Even Richard Gere would be shocked by this X-ray! Okay, we're joking. Actually, we have done extensive research on the Richard Gere gerbil urban legend and strongly believe it is false. Why would a man who used to be married to the supermodel Cindy Crawford need such a fetish? Many other celebrities have been victims of similar rumors, but since none have been verified, we remain skeptical.

Although our society likes to make these allegations about celebrities, this practice has been spoken of in urban legend for years. In fact, it even has a name: *gerbilling* (though our spell check did not recognize this word, go figure). The theory behind this action is that the gerbil's movements would sexually stimulate the prostate in males.

Although we do not know for sure, urban legend also says, that putting rodents up rectums was practiced as a form of torture in certain countries, most notably by Pinochet's regime in Chile. It was supposedly used as a method of torture because small rodents, when enclosed in a tight space, will aggressively claw their way out. We can imagine that the rodents' attempts to escape the space would be incredibly painful to the person in whom the gerbil was residing. For this reason we are highly skeptical that this was ever actually done as a sexual practice. Well, at least not twice by the same person!

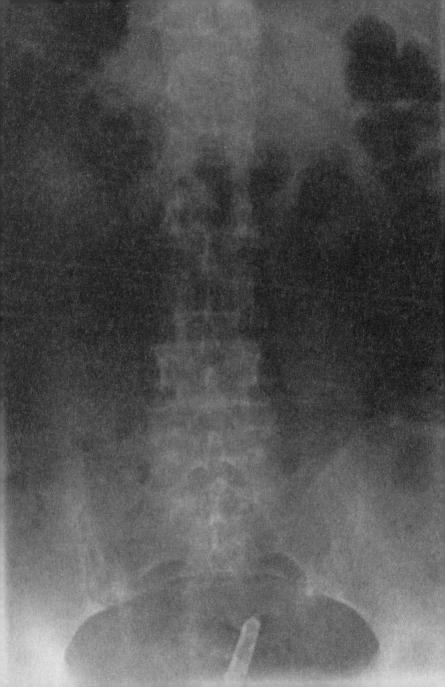

A Poor Way to Get Enough Minerals

We have found many unusual objects in the body, but seldom have we found something that still is in its basic mineral form. Obviously, the object didn't mineralize in this location despite the high pressures exerted by copious gas buildup thanks to two fantastic Mexican restaurants next to this patient's house. We asked the patient why he chose to stick quartz into himself. We wish we hadn't asked.

It turns out this patient was a mineralogist and way too obsessed with his work. He also did nothing to shatter the stereotypes of how exciting a mineralogist might be. He regaled us with how quartz, which is made up of one part silicon and four parts oxygen, is the second-most abundant mineral on earth, after feldspar. We didn't bother asking why he didn't choose feldspar, fearing he might tell us more about feldspar.

This patient did not just use regular quartz found in most rocks; he used something purer. Apparently, this sort of naturally pure quartz is not only rare but highly valuable, as it is used to develop silicon for semiconductors. The mineralogist saw this quartz as many people see gold or diamonds, namely just as valuable and beautiful. While we now understand the value of pure quartz to this patient, to us it's obvious that there are better places to store one's valuables.

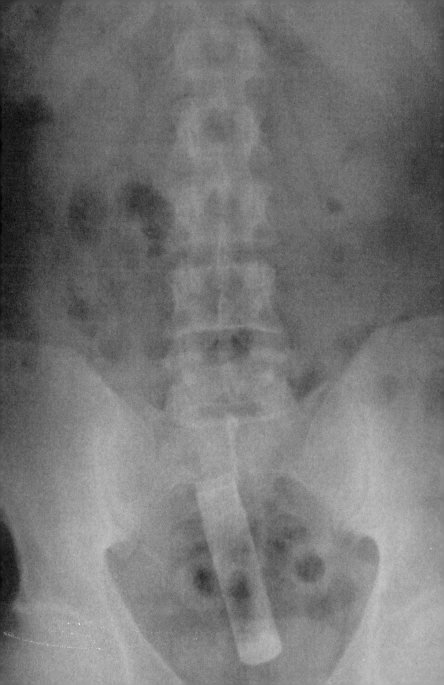

BACK TO SCHOOL

A Stick That's Often Stuck

Your mouth isn't the only thing people want to glue shut.

For many people, nothing captures the innocence of childhood like the humble glue stick. We hate to ruin the pleasant nostalgia, but the fact is that given its cylindrical shape and ubiquity, you had to see this coming up . . . or rather, going up.

Most commercial glue sticks are composed of glue made from nontoxic, acid-free, solvent-free ingredients, giving a rare instance where it's actually less risky to stick something commercial up your bum than one would think. Interestingly, there have been many documented cases of children, animals (such as dogs), and a few mentally disturbed adults eating glue sticks like popsicles. These creative eaters mostly experienced only mild, temporary symptoms like diarrhea. This effect occurs because the particles in the glue actually draw water from the gut by osmosis.

Of course, despite the nontoxic nature of the glue, the container or cap part of the glue stick can cause obstruction in the body if swallowed or inserted. That's why, just as you were taught in childhood, it's so important to put the cap of the glue back on. And you probably thought it was just so the glue wouldn't dry.

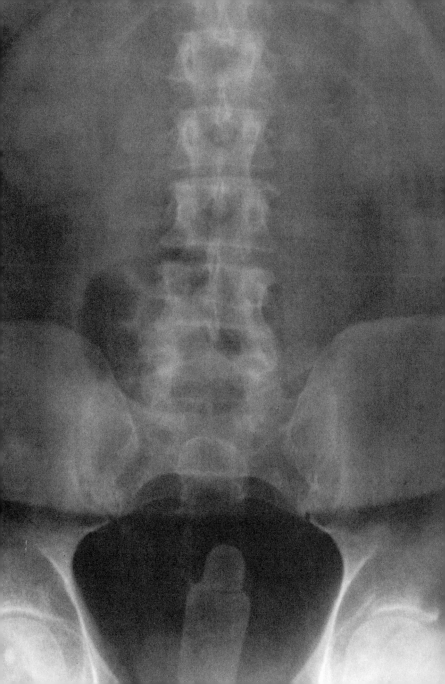

Not So Easy to Correct This Mistake

Liquid Paper was invented by Bette Nesmith Graham in the early 1950s. Famous for her now ubiquitous correctional fluid, Bette also produced a son, Michael Nesmith, who was one of the stars of the 1960s band The Monkees. We are not sure which would be more surprising for her to hear—that The Monkees did not always write and perform their own music early on, or that this bottle of correctional fluid was found where it was.

Another very off-label recreational use of correctional fluid has been as an inhalant. When individuals use inhalants, they breathe in fumes in an attempt to get high, but the effects of inhaling chemicals can be toxic and deadly. Similar to other inhalants, correctional fluid products are known to cause fatal arrhythmias, or irregular rhythms of the heart. So if you are attempting to do this, just stop and smell the roses instead.

An article about students inhaling correctional fluid stated, "School health officials, public health departments, and law enforcement personnel should be alerted to the need for surveillance of this type of activity." We say the same thing about *this* type of activity. Unfortunately, this bottle of correctional fluid was not found in the same person who had a pen up their rectum, which might have been useful. . . .

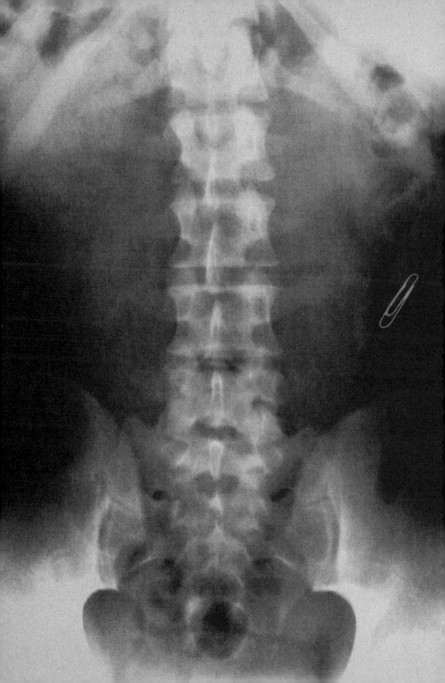

Of Cons and Clips

During an episode of *The Office*, Karen remarks to Creed, "You can't give paper clips to a baby. They might swallow them." To which Creed answers, "Oh, it's okay, I've got tons of them." However, as the case below demonstrates, paper-clip ingestion is no funny matter.

According to the Early Office Museum—as if most museums weren't boring enough—the early versions of the modern paper clip were created in the late 1800s and have been found everywhere from holding papers together to, if you are MacGyver, diffusing a bomb built by evildoers meant to blow up a building of innocent people. More realistically, though, paper clips are sometimes found inside the human body, perhaps as a misguided attempt to hold together "loose" bowel movements. Fortunately, most likely a swallowed paper clip will pass through the body without causing any harm, unless it was straightened . . . so stop straightening them just because you are bored.

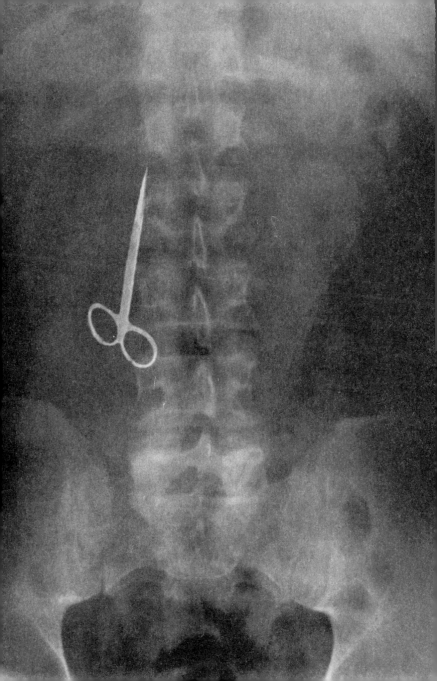

Maybe We Should Have Called This Book "Stuck In"

Cut it out? That's what got us here in the first place.

Nobody is perfect. Not even surgeons, despite what they may believe.

In his career, a surgeon might open the human body thousands of times and use tons of instruments, gauze, needles, and other objects, to perform a procedure in a bloody, difficult-to-visualize field. What could possibly go wrong? Eventually, no matter how good the surgeon is, an object will be left behind inside the body.

Although perfection in the operating room is not always possible, many steps are actually taken to avoid leaving objects inside the body, particularly in the operating room. One of the most advanced, state-of-the-art techniques to keep track of objects is—counting. All instruments and other objects are counted before and after the procedure to make sure they are accounted for. Also, almost all objects, even gauze, have a radio-opaque portion so that the item can easily be picked up on X-ray. This allows the error to be corrected more easily, and, as a bonus, it also provides us material for this book.

Not only does reducing this complication decrease lawsuits, but the hospitals also save money by not losing instruments. (Yes, we're joking . . . or are we?)

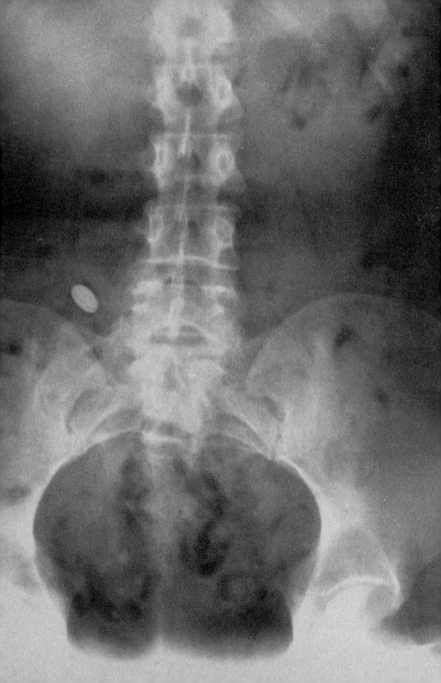

HARDWARE OR HARD *WHERE*?

Batteries Should Not Be Included

Over the last two decades batteries have become exceedingly small. The most popular small battery in use today is the button, or disc, battery. Most battery ingestions occur in children, who mistake these batteries for candy. However, there is a second peak of ingestion in the elderly, which makes sense since many elderly seem to have a harder time with newer technologies.

These batteries can contain a variety of caustic elements, such as lithium. As you might expect, there's no U.S. recommended daily allowance of lithium ions. The elements in batteries, given time to leak in the gastrointestinal tract, can cause a charged chemical reaction that produces sodium hydroxide, the main ingredient of bleach. Bleach may work wonders for cleaning clothes, but it is also highly toxic, and inside the body it can burn and create holes where they didn't exist before.

The most common area of obstruction is the end of the esophagus. If stuck there, the battery must be removed emergently by a specialist. If the battery does pass this point, passage can be expedited by a cathartic. Ironically, this method makes the patient and disc battery more like older, larger Energizer batteries, as they keep going and going and going and going . . .

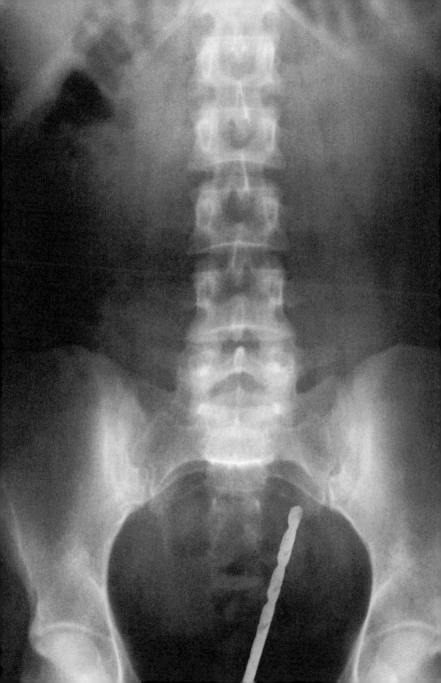

Drill, Baby, Drill!

As the price of oil rises, we understand the desperate desire to search for and extract oil from the nether regions, but this patient is pushing it.

Obviously, this case was an unfortunate accident. Like many accidents we see in the emergency department, alcohol was involved. Other effects of alcohol include making poor decisions, such as going to a Jonas Brothers concert as an adult or, well, ever. Another effect is taking on a task that a sober person would recognize that he or she has neither the skills nor the motivation to do, whether driving, drilling, or anything else. Unfortunately, the "Don't Drink and Drill" campaign never caught on, nor did the organization BADD, Builders Against Drunk Drilling.

In addition to auto accidents and drilling injuries, alcohol is responsible for over 4 million ER visits annually. This sobering fact has motivated some ERs to install specialized units for intoxicated individuals, or their own "drunk tank." Ultimately, between alcohol-related injuries, legal issues, and medical problems, the risks of drinking are self-evident. Although we enjoy sharing interesting medical scenarios such as this one, we do dream of a world in which they do not happen.

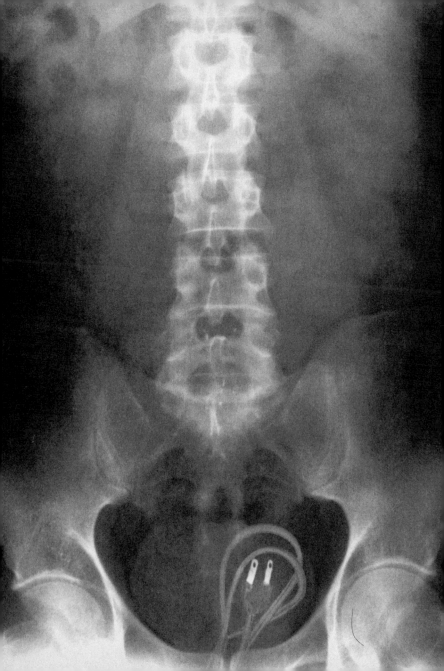

Shouldn't One Use an Adapter?

Since the time of Thomas Edison, all sorts of accidents have happened with electricity. When we tell kids not to play with electricity, though, this patient's case isn't what we mean. The question is, if the cord were hooked up, would this truly be dangerous?

When electricity flows in the body, heat is released; and if strong enough, this heat can damage whatever it's passing through. To get electricity to travel through the body is actually very difficult. Electricity tends to flow where there is least resistance. In fact, the fundamental electricity equation, Ohm's Law, describes electricity by Voltage (V) = Current (I) × (multiplied by) Resistance (R). Therefore, with a constant voltage, the higher the resistance, the lower the current will be. Since the body's organs have a very high resistance, the current tends to be quite low. You would not get much current flowing out of the body, either, no matter how powerful an ass some people seem to have.

The current, and the damage it causes, can be higher if the voltage is high, such as with lightning bolts, or if the resistance is low, such as in electrolyte-rich saliva. In other words, though putting the cord in the bottom end was not a good idea, it was still better than inserting it in the top end, which would have been a real shocker.

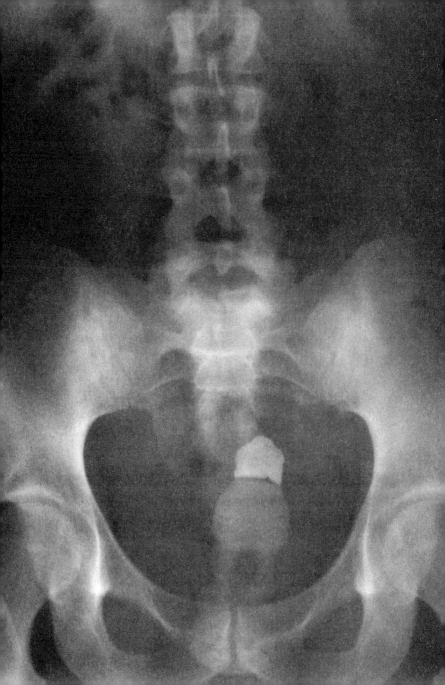

Not So Bright Idea

One argument for making the change from incandescent bulbs to compact fluorescent lightbulbs (CFLs) is the smaller amount of energy consumed by CFLs. In this person's case, there may have been another reason, since doing this probably took quite an amount of energy, although apparently not much brightness.

The Environmental Protection Agency (EPA) states that mercury in a CFL is in the form of a vapor, most of which is bound to the inside of the bulb as it is used. When broken, approximately 14 percent of the total mercury (the unbound portion) is released into the air as vapor. The vapor form carries the elemental form of mercury, which is not well absorbed in the gastrointestinal tract and therefore less likely to cause toxicity. This good news for the patient was merely blind luck, since clearly no lightbulb went off in his head when he thought of doing this.

Take-home point: Switch from traditional incandescent lightbulbs to CFLs, and, remember, there is a big difference between screwing in the bulb and screwing the bulb.

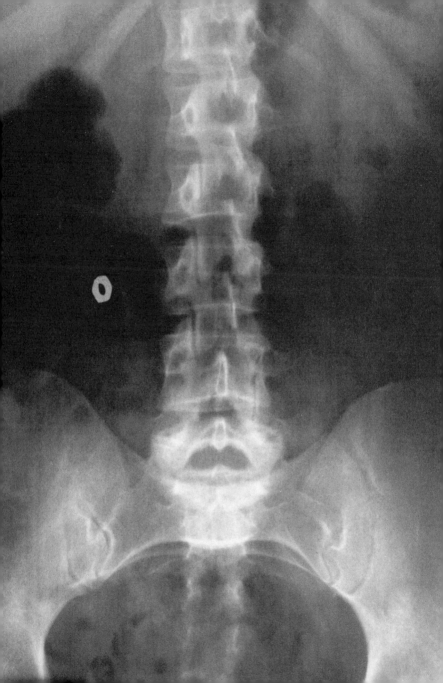

The Nutty Case of a Nut in a Nutcase

Here is something you've probably been waiting for: a case of swallowed nuts. We often see swallowed nuts in the ER. Patients can't seem to help swallowing their nuts, other people's nuts, or just random nuts they find on the street.

If small, swallowed nuts will usually pass through the throat and rectum without difficulty, although as they mix with electrolyte-rich saliva they often get salty along the way. When you have nuts made of steel (insert your own Superman joke here), sometimes magnets have been used to facilitate their removal.

One of the more memorable cases regarding nuts involved a seventeen-year-old boy who swallowed several nuts and bolts. Eventually he was discharged from the hospital, and he passed the objects. An otherwise boring case except for his explanation as to why he had done it: He "felt like a change of scenery." In other words, this patient swallowed these objects to achieve *secondary gain*, which is to obtain something material, such as being in the hospital instead of prison or juvenile hall. Secondary gain can also include shelter, food, medication, money, etc. All this kid really gained was being considered, well, nuts.

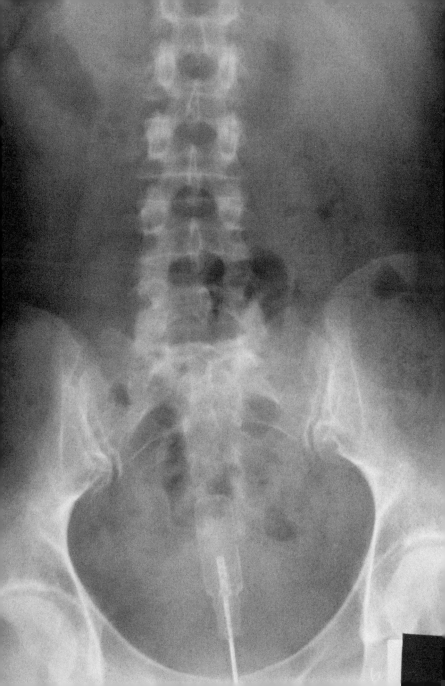

I Meant, "Can I Have Orange Juice and Vodka?"

No, this patient wasn't actually ordering a screwdriver drink. This patient did not even have access to alcohol, since he was incarcerated.

In this case, the patient said he somehow ran into a screwdriver. When asked how he found a screwdriver, he gave us a pretty screwy answer by saying that he was just minding his own business when someone told him to go screw himself.

Most penetrating assault wounds are to the stomach, with the greatest risk of injury to the liver because of the liver's size, followed by the bowel. Luckily, this screwdriver missed everything. We even checked to see if he had any screws in his body, since now even screws are used to repair bones and stimulate bone growth around them. Go figure, no screws were to be found.

Because of the clean nature of this injury, we could not help but wonder if the patient inserted this screwdriver into his own body to temporarily go to a medical ward. Ultimately, this patient left us with more questions than answers. Whether the patient did this to himself or was a victim of jail violence, we knew that there was nothing we could do to prevent a recurrence. Unfortunately, the patient was doubly screwed.

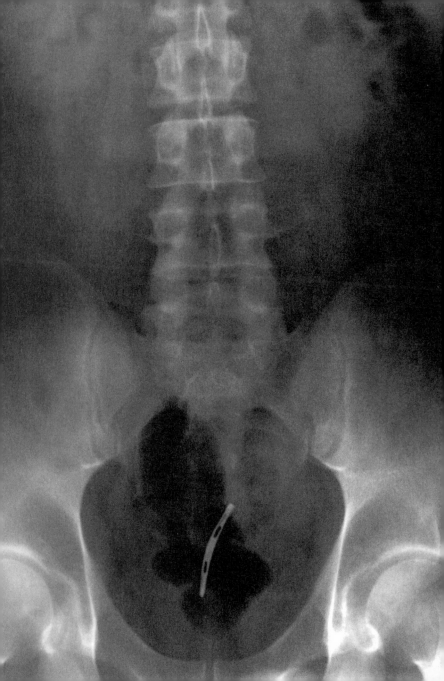

LOW-END FASHION

A Barber and a Surgeon Walk into a Little Bar

Many people don't realize that hair is found only in mammals and is a feature used to define the mammalian class. Perhaps that's why we think the more hair you have the more of an animal you are. Take that, Dad!

One of the more humble and cheaper, yet indispensable, hair maintenance products is the barrette, which is simply a fancier name for a hair clip. The word *barrette* is French and means "a little bar," which is also probably where this patient was before this incident happened.

Although this patient may have been of drinking age, barrettes are more commonly swallowed by younger children. In adults, accidental barrette ingestion is less common, but nonetheless, the situation can end up being just as hairy. In such situations professional help is often required. To be clear, by professional we mean a doctor or a surgeon, not a barber, even though once upon a time surgeons and barbers were the same. But that's a story for another time.

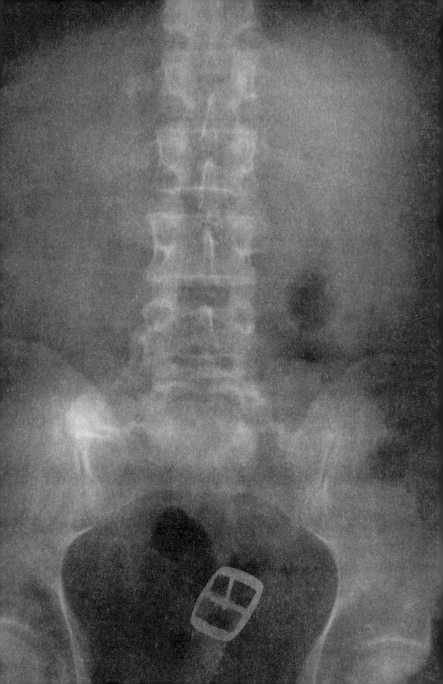

No Championship Belt Earned Here

Since the Bronze Age and throughout most of history, belts have served a more decorative function. Being worn higher on the body, they completely avoided proximity to certain orifices. It wasn't until the early 1900s, when the waistlines of trousers were lowered on the body, that belts were considered to serve a purpose beyond style. Now the belt's most common use is to prop up pants, with the exception of certain teenage boys and hip-hop singers who are still not familiar with this practice.

Today, belt uses have progressed from holding up pants to holding all sorts of tools and gadgets, from the handyman, whose belt often seems to be there just for the tools and not so much for the pants, to Batman, who we are not even sure wears pants. We can now add one more use to the list. This patient explained that because of the belt's adjustable length and long shape, it would be easy to retrieve when necessary. He became very embarrassed when he realized that he could not open the buckle by himself, as it eluded his reach. Those airplane instructions to simply lift up the buckle to release the belt no longer seemed so easy to follow.

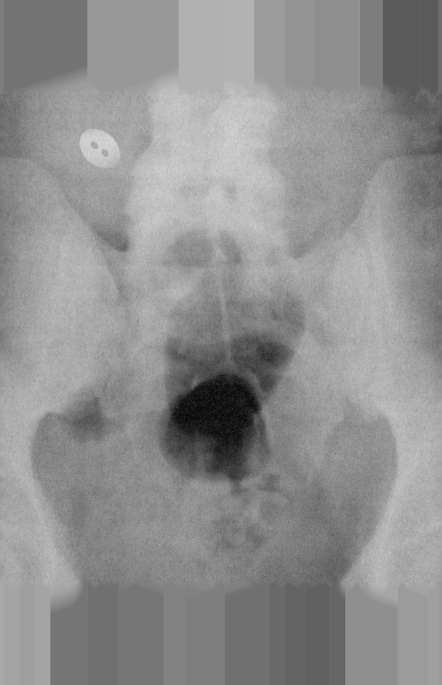

A Way Innie

This patient had a wonderful collection of winter coats that, oddly, had no buttons. His mother was very curious about what happened to those little fasteners. Well, we found them. Of course, it was where parents often think to look last, but we often look first: The child's stomach.

The only "button" that is designed to be on or in the body is the belly button. The navel marks the area of the body to which the umbilical cord was connected. To aid in the elimination of urine, the fetal bladder is connected to a canal that joins with the umbilical cord. If that canal does not close after birth, it is called an opening in the urachus, not to be confused with an opening in your anus, as if that hasn't already gotten enough attention in our patients.

If the urachus does remain open, the belly button becomes like these buttons . . . a way innie.

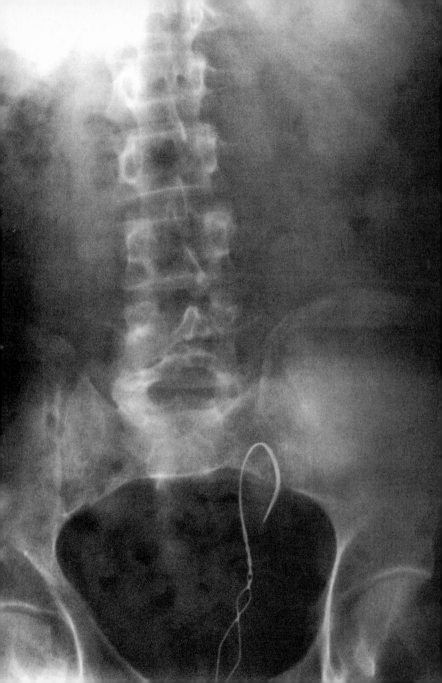

Not Enough Room in Your Closet?

It's hard to hang loose during a situation like this. This patient had to hang tight as his physicians figured out a plan to remove the wire hanger. The doctors wanted to attempt manipulation by hand, which, if you think about it, is what got the patient into trouble in the first place. They did not want to be too aggressive, considering the pointy end of the hanger could cause some serious damage.

The first step was to do what physicians often have to do when removing hard, wire objects from the body. They had to remove all the excess wire so it wouldn't be in their way. This practice is more commonly done with objects like fishhooks embedded in the skin, and it is the reason why most emergency departments have wire cutters.

Cutting wires does come with a risk, since the great force it takes to cut the wire can cause the two ends to immediately move outward after being cut. In this case, moving outward meant moving inward, so the head of the hanger had to be held by grippers while the cutting was taking place. Once the base of the hanger was removed and no longer in the way, removing the hook of the hanger was even easier than getting it in there.

After the closet hanger situation was dealt with, the ER doctors instructed the patient to use dresser drawers instead.

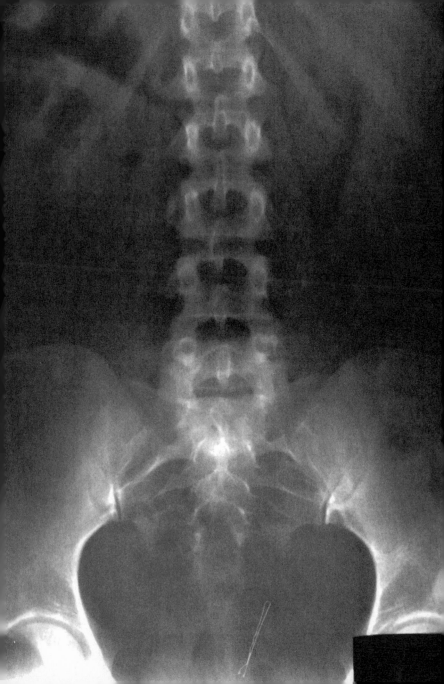

When You Just Need Something to Hold Things Together

Hairpins are easy to store and easy to lose, although this is not usually where they are stored when they are lost.

Although hairpins look and even sound sharp because of the word, *pin*, most hairpins actually have blunted ends and typically do not harm the bowel. Most hairpins usually pass on their own despite their length. In fact, studies have evaluated the size of objects that can be swallowed and passed compared to the size of objects that will fail to pass. Yes, this was studied.

Objects larger than approximately 5 cm × 2 cm, or for Americans who like to swallow objects, 2 in. × 0.8 in., tend to not pass. Smaller objects tend to pass on their own—although they might still need to be dealt with by a doctor prior to passing if the objects are sharp or corrosive. In other words, don't start swallowing things just because they are below the cutoff. No object meets the size requirements for this ride.

Obviously, individual objects and bowels are unique, but the quoted dimensions above predict what *most likely* will happen. Perhaps it's the willpower of the person and object that create the exceptions in those cases when an unstoppable force meets an immovable object. Or maybe the patient just eats a lot of fiber.

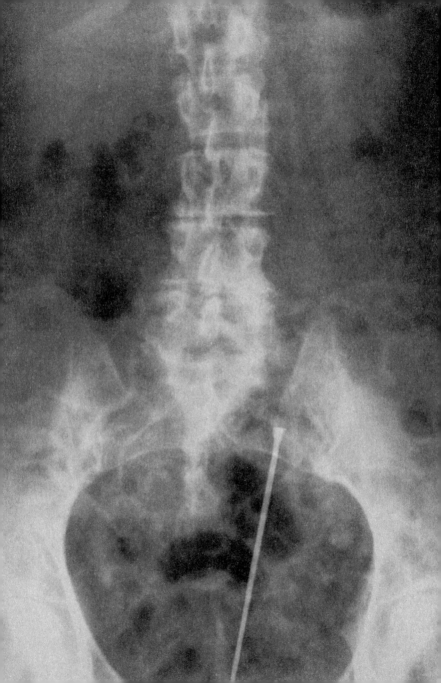

Knits and Nitwits

Given their function, one usually sees knitting needles in the hands of women and sometimes men. However, once in a while, a knitting needle makes its appearance *inside* the body. The possible explanations given usually are that either the knitting got boring—and based on our observations of knitting, that must be true—or occasionally knitters are just looking for something *else* to do with their hands.

Because of all the risks, we recommend to such patients that they abandon their efforts to knit their own clothing and stick with the BeDazzler. We could not find any injuries involving bedazzling, despite our best efforts . . . but please don't take this as a challenge to prove us wrong, and definitely leave the Shake Weight at home, too.

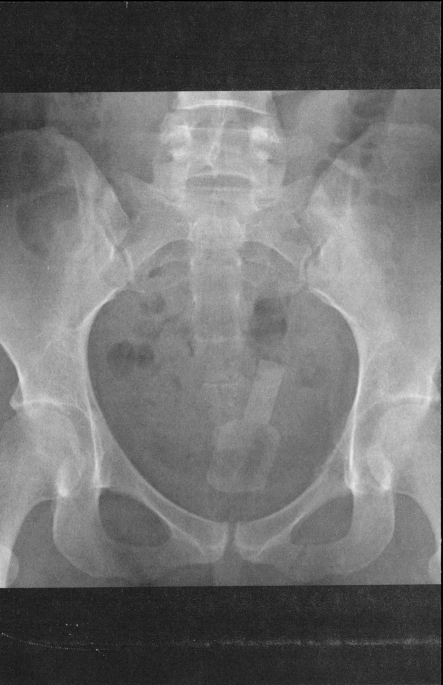

What's the Right Shade for This?

Nail polish is most often used as a decorative paint for toenails and fingernails. This person completely missed the mark . . . literally.

It would take more than acetone to remove this nail polish. Acetone is also a chemical produced in our body when we are unable to metabolize sugar as a weaker alternative source of energy. This process is most often seen in cases of starvation or malnutrition, such as with alcoholics, diabetics who cannot absorb sugar, and, in all seriousness, those on the Atkins diet. If enough acetone is produced, one's breath may smell like nail polish remover. In other words, in theory, at least, if this person starved herself of sugar, she might be able to remove the nail polish on her own.

Because of metabolic processes such as those noted above, premedical and medical students must thoroughly learn complex organic chemistry in courses so difficult that often many students are "weeded out." Who would have thought that we'd be applying that knowledge in this situation, though truly, no chemical equation will help this patient.

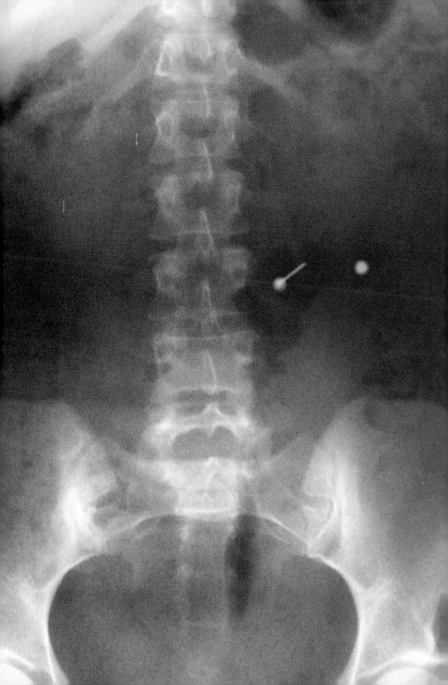

A Slip Off *the Tongue*

Woody Allen famously said, "How can I believe in God when just last week I got my tongue caught in the roller of an electric typewriter?" Given that the electric typewriter has gone extinct, we expect the tongues of the world are safe from this kind of predicament.

However, doctors continue to see other kinds of trauma involving the tongue, including complications from tongue piercing. Along with its increased popularity has come increased awareness of its complications, including severe pain (Duh!), infection, nerve damage, swelling leading to swallowing and breathing problems in severe cases, excessive bleeding, chipped teeth, and other dental problems. Although these are all serious, in this book, the most important complication is something getting stuck or swallowed.

Such a case was reported a few years ago and involved a sixteen-year-old girl. She was wearing a tongue ring with no clip that slipped off her tongue while eating, and she accidentally swallowed it. She had an abdominal X-ray, which showed not only the tongue ring, but also the clip! She then admitted that she had accidentally swallowed the clip of the tongue ring the day before. Now that was tough to swallow.

For this teenager's recklessness, she got a tongue-lashing.

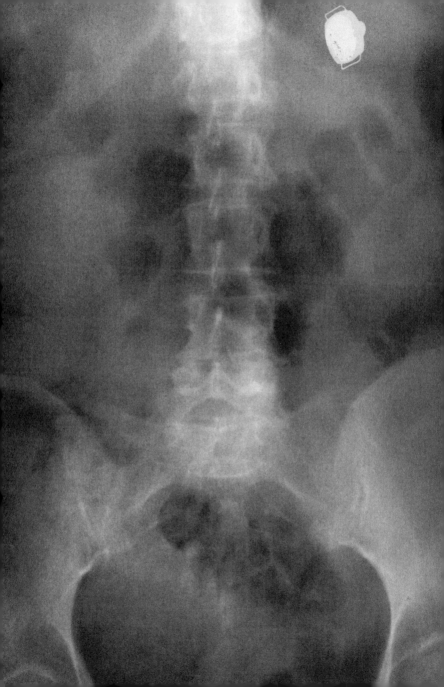

The End of Time

In the movie *Pulp Fiction,* Captain Koons tells Butch the story of Butch's father's watch. While in a P.O.W. camp, Butch's father hid the watch in his rectum for five years to keep it from being discovered by enemy soldiers. He died of dysentery in the camp but gave the watch to Captain Koons, who hid it in his own rectum for two years. As fantastic as this story may sound, it is possible for a watch to survive in the human body without permanent damage to either the watch or the body. Doesn't mean you'd want to keep the watch, though.

There are many more reports of people swallowing watches than inserting them. In 1902, actress Maud Lillian Berri "nearly fainted as a result of severe pains throughout her body, and particularly in the intestines." An X-ray revealed a small watch in her stomach. Apparently she had fallen asleep with the watch in her hand, and, while asleep, somehow had put it in her mouth and swallowed it. Another case involved a man with a psychiatric disorder, who, while being mugged, hid his watch in his mouth and swallowed it. The watch remained in his stomach for nearly five months. When the watch was removed, it was found to be intact and ticking. Since accidental swallowing of watches is such a frequent occurrence, you now know why wristwatches were invented.

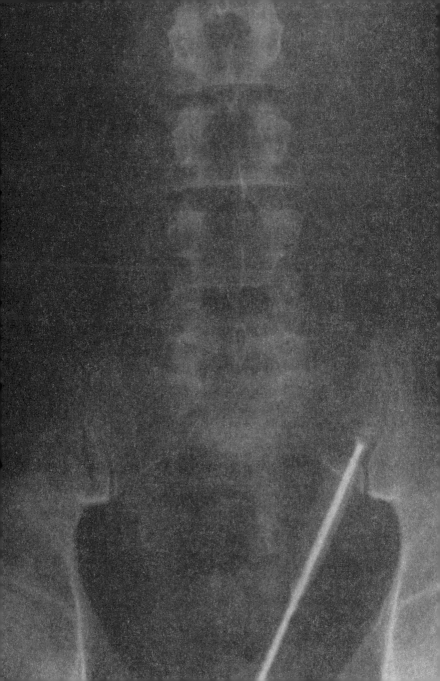

WEAPONS OF [M]ASS DESTRUCTION

Bull's-Eye!

You may have noticed a few things about this X-ray. First, Cupid really missed the mark on this one! The arrow missed the heart and entered through "the exit ramp" instead. Secondly, the arrow has remained straight in a place that has more twists and turns than an episode of *Lost*. This is not surprising, given the rigid material of the arrow, but what is surprising is the lack of evidence of a perforated bowel in this case.

In total, the gastrointestinal tract is approximately twenty feet long in a living adult. Fitting this much of anything in the human body will require some folding, which makes it more likely that sharp objects will pierce the multiple folds of tissue in the abdominal cavity.

Some people have asked us about other graphic arrow injuries. There are reports of arrows going through a patient's head, called by one group of physicians a "William Tell" injury. These types of injuries can be particularly dangerous, since the central nervous system has a rather limited ability to heal. For this reason, injuries to the brain and spinal cord can be devastating. There's often no way to replace what is lost. So how do people survive these injuries? Some people believe this is because we use only less than 5 percent of our brains, a theory that may seem quite obvious to anyone who has ever watched *Jersey Shore*.

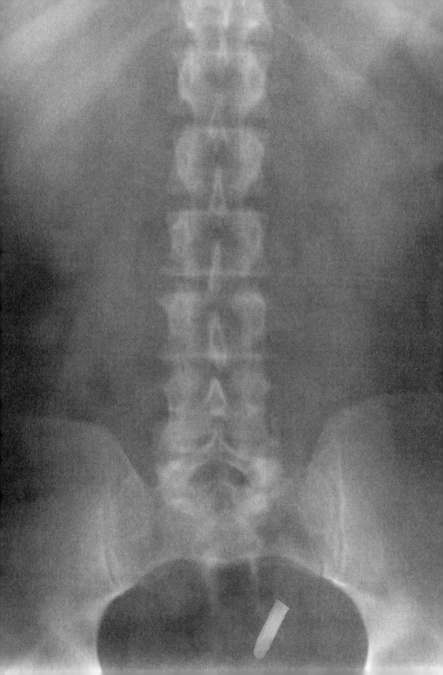

Right on Target

Bullets have a long history of use in warfare. The silver bullet, however, has a special place in folklore. Legends tell of its ability to kill werewolves. The silver bullet was the Lone Ranger's signature weapon, while Coors Light has been known by this name long before the mountains on the label turned blue when the beer becomes cold. A lesser-known use of the term is in reference to Preparation H suppositories. This unfortunate patient became quite confused when his doctor suggested he use a silver bullet suppository to help him move his bowels.

Oftentimes, patients are shot in the buttocks by rival gangs as a sign of disrespect, although we don't know where exactly one would shoot to show respect. If a patient were actually shot by a bullet in the rectum, the force of the bullet would cause a lot of damage, which is not evident on this X-ray. Therefore we can draw the conclusion that such an item was placed there more gingerly.

During the second season of the show *Grey's Anatomy*, a patient had unexploded ammunition from a homemade bazooka inside his abdomen. One of the show's characters was required to reach into the patient to steady the ammunition to avoid an explosion. On the show, the explosive was not lodged in the patient's bottom. The producers are probably saving that for sweeps week.

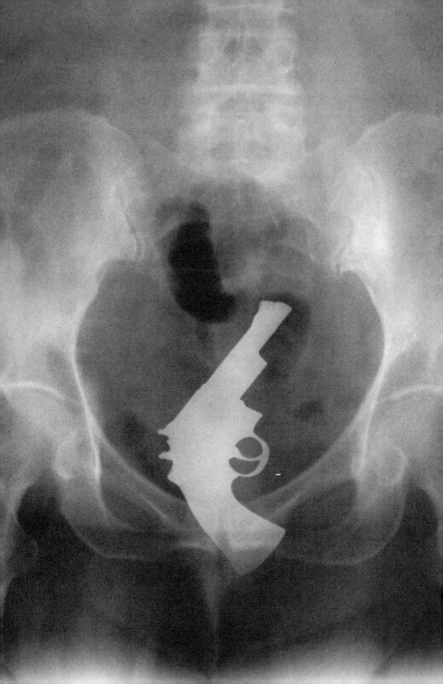

Guns Don't Do This, People Do This

A gun up a rectum seems absolutely impossible at first, but we are constantly amazed at the lengths people go to make the seemingly impossible possible. After reviewing the anatomy, we better understood how this feat was accomplished. Guns may shoot straight, but their shapes are somewhat curved, like the rectum. Yes, rectums are supposed to be curved if you are checking yourself.

If you make a curved motion that follows the same path as the rectum, the insertion can be successfully completed. Such placement would require facing the handle and barrel of the gun toward the front, positioning the cylinder away, and curving the gun counterclockwise from the perspective of the patient's right side while facing the patient. It sounds easy, right? Remember, this is just a description, not instructions!

This doesn't answer the much more puzzling question of why on earth someone would consider doing this. Inserting objects in the rectal vault is already dangerous enough, but a gun! Could this have been a strange suicide attempt?

Actually, this was purely recreational. Some people really do love their guns. It makes you wonder where certain people would stand on this practice. Many conservatives love limiting this sort of behavior, but then again, many conservatives also loathe any sort of gun control.

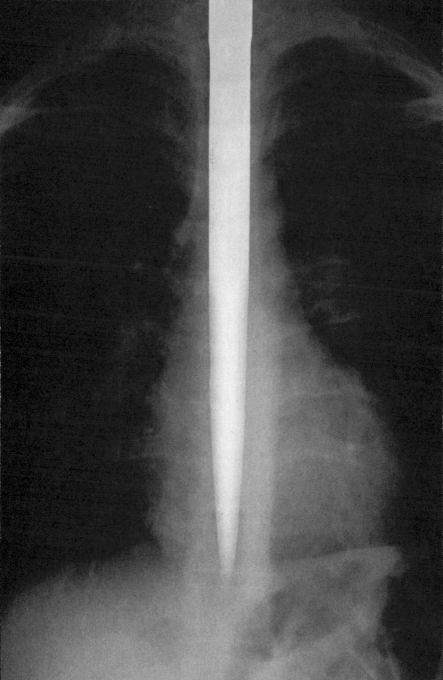

Went Down Smooth

Although thinking of swallowing somebody's sword sounds dirty, it's been done for over 4,000 years. The basic concept is to insert a long sword down the throat without causing any damage to oneself. The actual practice is anything but basic, since it comes with the high risk of injury one might expect from taking a sharp, long blade designed for causing harm and purposely inserting it near vital organs.

Part of the technique for swallowing swords involves hyperextending the neck and controlling one's gag reflex as the sword passes through the esophageal sphincter. Saliva further lubricates the sword as it continues to pass inches away from the aorta, heart, and many other structures, which, if injured, could result in instant death.

Estimates suggest that there are less than 50 active sword-swallowers in the world, half of whom are probably being either admitted to or discharged from a hospital or psychiatric institution at any given time. Some world records for sword swallowing include swallowing over 38,000 swords in one year (that's over 100 swords daily) and 50 swords at once. Most people would rather stick with striving to set the record for eating most hot dogs at the local county fair—a practice that is almost as dangerous in the long run as sword swallowing, given what is in a hot dog these days.

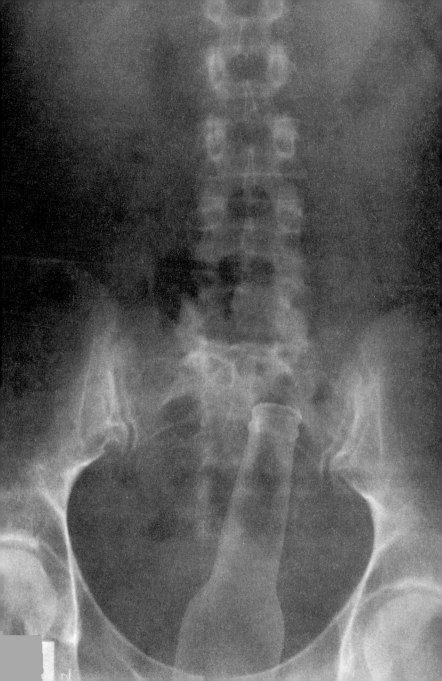

JUST CHILLIN'

Beer Before Liquor Gets You to This Point Quicker

Considering how many examples of bottle insertion we have, seeing a patient who has placed a bottle in his rectum is not a surprise to the surgeons who operate in these cases. The surprise comes when the bottle is removed and the physicians learn what is contained in the bottle. Very often, as you probably can guess, it's alcohol.

A patient's blood alcohol level (BAL) is typically measured by a blood test or breathalyzer, although in this patient's case, perhaps by passing gas. Depending on what this patient had for dinner, the police may decide to file additional charges.

If a patient is a long-standing alcoholic, he may develop damage to the liver, blood vessels, skin, and brain. Some patients also develop visual hallucinations of small people, called *Lilliputian hallucinations*, a reference to the tiny characters in Jonathan Swift's novel *Gulliver's Travels*. Perhaps it was the little people who placed this bottle where it was.

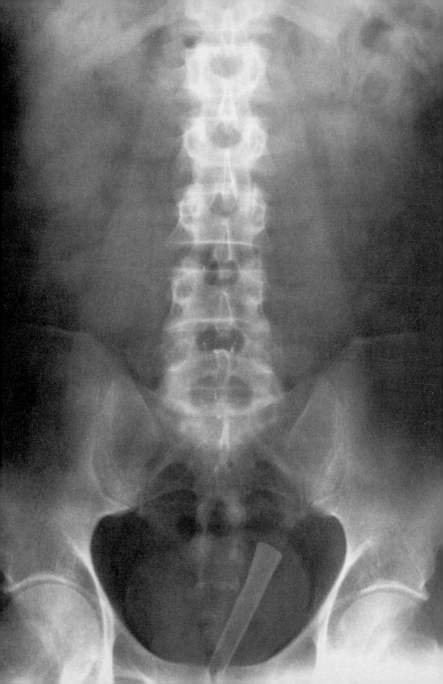

Super High or Stupid Guy?

Former U.S. president Bill Clinton famously admitted to trying marijuana, but reported that he did not inhale. Well, here is a case of a patient who smoked crack cocaine and not only inhaled the drug, but swallowed the pipe, too!

The image of drug users being chased by the police is quite common, with a number of the suspects trying to destroy the evidence, rather than getting caught with it. This is what happened in this case as well, except the patient apparently took it a little too far.

We do know that sharing pipes can result in the spreading of bacteria and viruses from one user to another, including the spread of tuberculosis. We can't imagine the bacteria this patient could spread. Finally, a lesser-known danger of smoking crack that you may not have heard about.

We imagine this situation could have been avoided even if the individual had the crack pipe but just hadn't used it, since his intoxication likely affected his decision making. There's nothing high-end about this story; just a high ending.

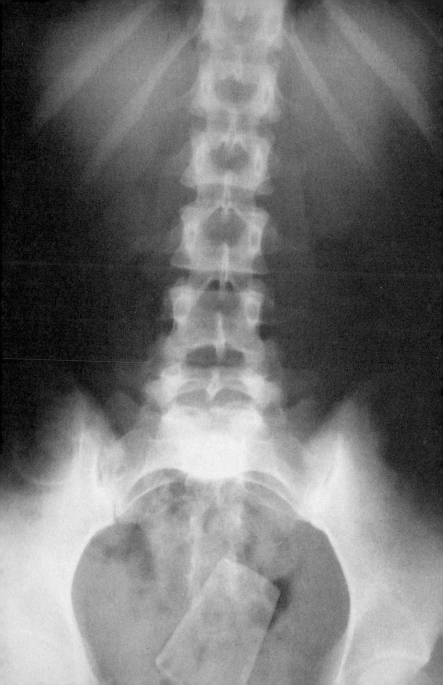

Bottoms Up!

We have seen many arguments over just how much liquor one gets in a single shot. Apparently there is no standard size in the United States, except in Utah where a single shot consists of 1.5 fluid ounces, and here we thought no one even drank alcohol in Utah. In the rest of America, the amount usually ranges from 1.25 to 1.5 fluid ounces. Again, who would have thought that shot glasses are the biggest in Utah? Perhaps this amount is considered a "family-size" serving?

One of the unforeseen risks with the shot glass actually comes not from the liquor in it, but the decorations on it, as they can contain lead. As discussed elsewhere in this book, lead poisoning can cause stomach pain, muscle and joint pains, kidney problems, headaches, memory problems, anemia, and decreased libido. This latter problem probably makes you want to keep the shot glass as far away from your genital area as you can. Once again, who would have thought that Utah would sell glasses that might cause that potential problem?

As for how to explain this patient's shot glass up his bottom, this must have been the patient's own version of "Bottoms up!"

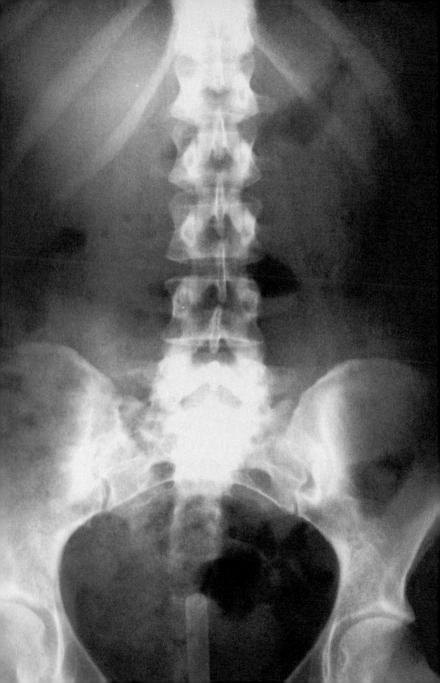

Please Drink Responsibly

Many of the cases we discuss involve alcohol and the bottom. You can't get drunk from putting alcohol in your bottom, though. Or can you? Hopefully you are interested, but not *too* interested.

While pouring or sticking a bottle full of alcohol in the rectum may be ineffective for the purpose of getting drunk, one common practice we see is the use of tampons soaked in vodka and inserted into the vagina. This method is most common in young women who are trying to get drunk without having the smell of alcohol on their breath revealed to parents or law enforcement officials. Clever girls, since vaginas don't need to produce legal identification, although we hear rumors that impending legislation in Arizona may change that.

The use of alcohol at a young age is not recommended and can lead to very dangerous situations. Research has shown that adolescent brains are not developed enough to fully consider the long-term consequences of their actions, evident to anyone who's ever spent more than ninety seconds with a teenager. Eventually this inability to consider long-term consequences leads to disturbing results, like the Spice Girls becoming the bestselling girl group of all time.

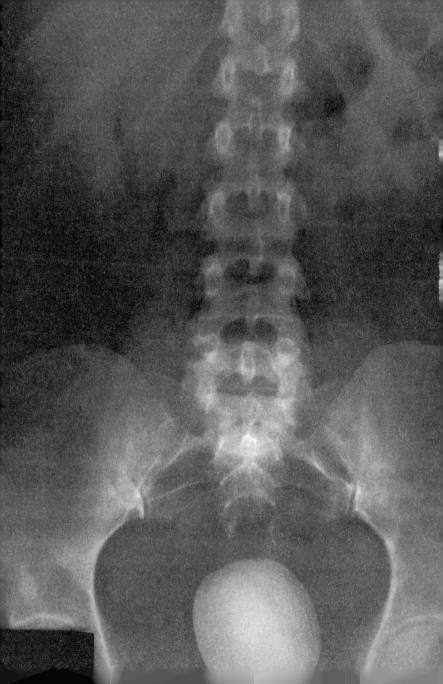

'Snuff Said

Chewing tobacco is *usually* placed in one's mouth between the gum and the cheek or between the lower lip and the gumline below the front teeth. The nicotine can also cause increased salivation, which makes us wonder about the effect of inserting it in one's rectum.

Chewing tobacco may result in the development of cancer of the esophagus, mouth, lip, throat, cheek, gum, and/or tongue. Trying to treat oral cancers can result in significant disfigurement and death. So ultimately, for this individual, it may have been safer to place the entire sealed tin of chewing tobacco where he did, as opposed to putting the tobacco itself in his mouth. Some doctors may applaud this patient's decision to not chew or smoke the tobacco, but others would say that such praise would just be blowing smoke up his ass.

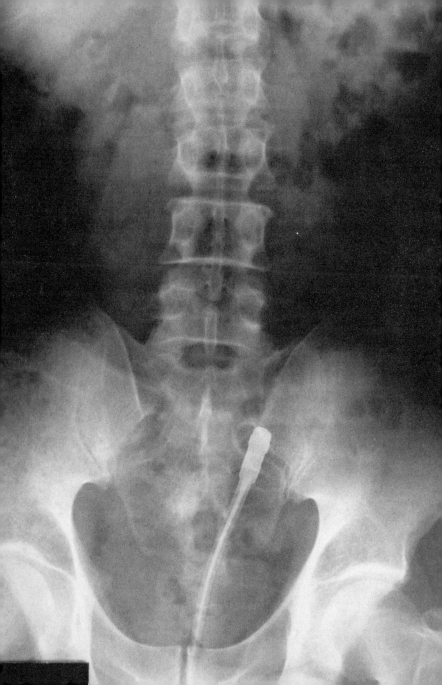

LOW TECH

Want Even More Channels?

It's hard to believe that just thirty years ago we were limited to about five TV channels. Now, with the proliferation of cable and satellite television, people can choose among literally hundreds of different channels to flip through and still find nothing worthwhile to watch. We are glad this person at least used a cable rather than a satellite dish.

Fortunately for this patient, cables are surrounded by either a rubber or, more commonly, a plastic coating. Although the coating has protective features for this patient, the true purpose of the coating is to protect the wire from many threats, including ultraviolet (UV) or fire damage; not an issue here unless the patient recently ate Mexican or Indian. The heavy insulation aims to prevent the loss of the transmitted cable signal and also helps to deter electromagnetic interference, which can cause static on the television screen image. Doctors often wish they had similar heavy insulation around their noses to actually create interference with the flatulence that can be emitted from cases like this.

Although the coating may increase image quality, many believe the multiple viewing options now available have eroded the quality of the programming. Basically, there's only a bunch of crap on cable.

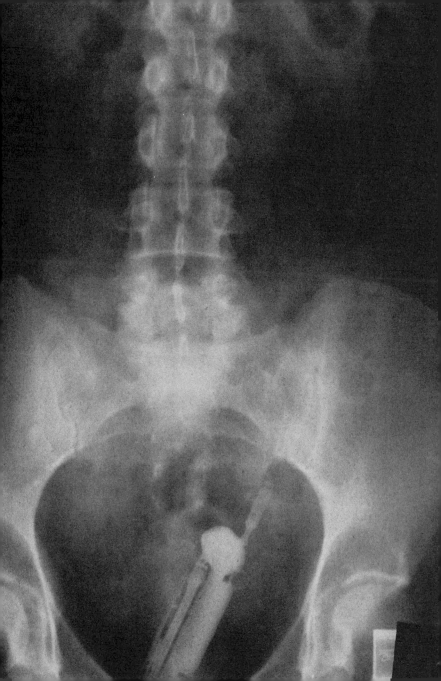

Reach Out and Touch Someone

There may be some debate on whether the iPhone or an Android is better for rectal stimulation. Regardless, we recommend shutting off the camera.

Yes, this person was actually found to have a cellular phone in his rectum. Not surprisingly, the phone was on vibrate mode. We suppose this is one way to ensure you never miss a call.

In this case, when the phone was removed, we found that there was a call waiting. The patient said he must have been constipated. Fortunately, he was able to get back in touch with the caller, since he qualified for his phone carrier's " 'Ends and Family" program.

Phone manufacturers deny an association between this practice and rectal cancer, although it might have been safer to stick a headset up there. We recommend that those who insert headsets in their rear not stick their heads up there as well, although some people seem unable to refrain from doing so, whether or not a headset is present.

Can you hear me now? Good!

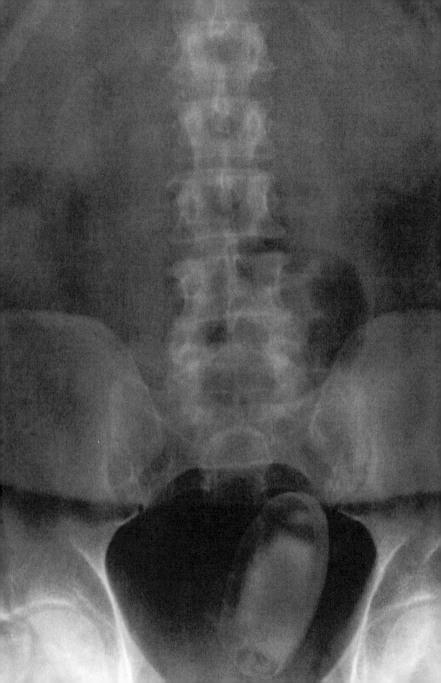

Good Thing He Didn't Upgrade to Wireless

We've found a lot of electronic gadgets in this part of the body, but most of these gadgets were designed to be inserted into the anus. A computer mouse in this location, however, gives a new meaning to the word, "technosexual."

This patient thought the mouse would be easy to remove since it already had a cord attached. With the tracking ball acting as a wheel, though, the mouse became far too mobile for this user. We knew the tracking ball effect would decrease with time since, like all tracking balls, it would pick up some debris, especially in this environment. But the patient stated he didn't have the luxury of time because of an unanticipated side effect.

Apparently, per the patient, the tightness and pressure within the rectum led to an unanticipated clicking of the mouse. This unpredictable clicking, again per the patient, accidentally took the patient's Internet browser to "dirty" Web sites. He explained that he was just not that kind of person and wanted the device removed as promptly as possible so he could resume his clean, except for the mouse, life.

We recommended that the patient use laptop and keyboard touch pads, emphasizing what is supposed to touch the pad.

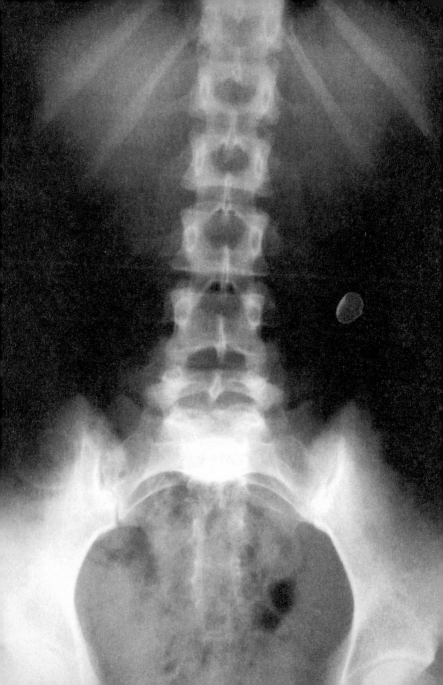

See Nothing, Say Nothing, Hear Nothing

Portable audio players have radically changed over the years, while earphones have also seen their own evolution. Now small enough for the ear canals, earphones are also small enough for other openings of the body.

A nine-month-old boy was brought to the ER after his parents noticed that the earphones he had in his mouth were missing one of the metallic mesh pieces. An X-ray revealed the mesh piece in the upper esophagus, which fortunately could be removed using optical grasping forceps. Although the swallowing of earphone pieces is a problem, the issue of potential hearing loss for millions of people who use earphones remains a bigger challenge. For years, listening to bands, such as Led Zeppelin, The Who, and Nirvana, too loudly has been blamed for hearing loss. On the other hand, given how unavoidable the music of Celine Dion and Michael Bolton is in our culture, fans of the aforementioned rock bands are likely quite thankful for their hearing loss.

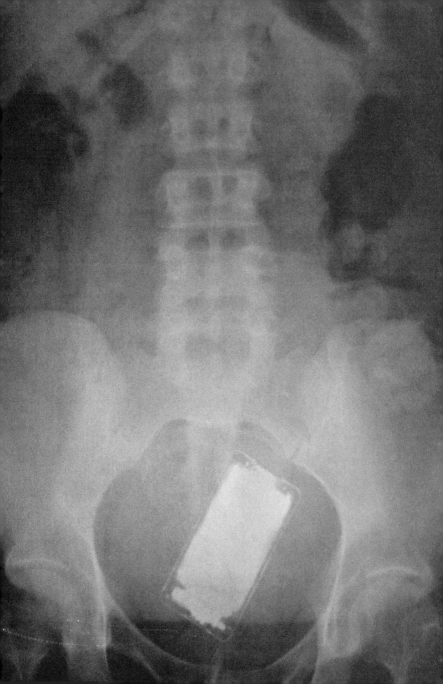

Why They Invented the Nano

Initially, this patient complained of unusual "musical" flatulence after meals, which seemed to vary depending on what he ate. For instance, he thought he heard Andrea Bocelli after Italian meals, Enrique Iglesias after Mexican food, and Tim McGraw after consuming barbecue chicken. Similarly, as the patient recently struggled more and more, hoping for something a little more than just "Blowin' in the Wind," all he could get was Rage Against the Machine. We wonder whether a smaller iPod in his body would have moved more quickly through him, perhaps while playing "Band on the Run."

Upon removal of the device, the surgeons reported hearing Men at Work singing, "I come from the land down under."

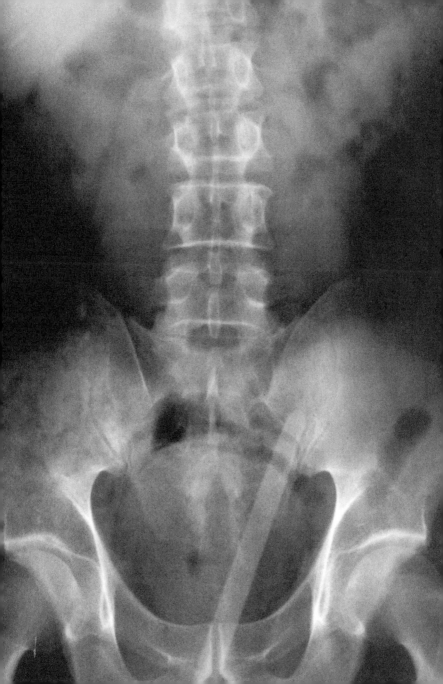

LOVEY-DOVEY

Some Candles Should Not Be Burned at Either End

Although the candle has largely been supplanted by electric lights, the candle continues to show up in places where, as we have said many times, "the sun don't shine." In addition to its starring role here in the human gut, the candle has also been at the center of many religious ceremonies, romantic overtures, and birthday cakes. This all adds up to yearly sales of about $2 billion, according to the National Candle Association. Even more amazing, there is a National Candle Association.

Scent is the most frequent purchasing factor mentioned by candle buyers, although this patient apparently didn't care very much about scent. Needless to say, the physician removing the candle certainly did. In the United States, consumers can choose from nearly 10,000 different scents, which are just enough to allow all the U.S. allergy specialists to afford sending their children to private schools, buy a new Mercedes every other year, and still take a yearly family vacation in the Swiss Alps. Records indicate that as far back as 3000 BC the Egyptians were using candles made of beeswax and other natural fats. Since this was also the time when the pharaoh kingdom was formed, the humble candle must have been used to light the deep, dark recesses of the great pyramids and temples long before it was found in this deep, dark recess.

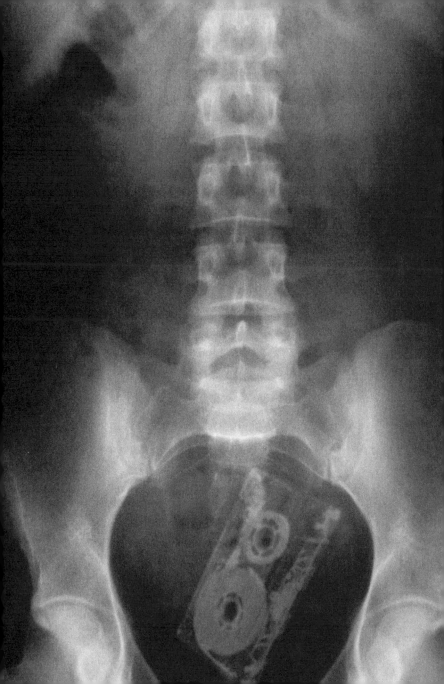

Don't Record This

At least it wasn't an 8-track.

In the 1980s and 1990s, there was no better way to say, "I love you," than to make a mixtape for someone. This has all changed since the advent of the CD burner and the MP3 player. While we have found an MP3 player in the same place, we're still looking for a CD burner.

The cassette revolution was not without controversy, as the music industry was particularly concerned that "dubbing" would limit consumer purchasing of prerecorded music. These debates only seem to repeat themselves with each new recording media. The recording industry never warned us of this, though; nor did we warn the industry.

Although we were never able to confirm the playlist, one can imagine this mixtape containing such greats as Sir Mix-A-Lot's "Baby Got Back," Wreckx-N-Effect's "Rump Shaker," LL Cool J's "Big Ole Butt," and, of course, the Stealers Wheel classic "Stuck in the Middle with You."

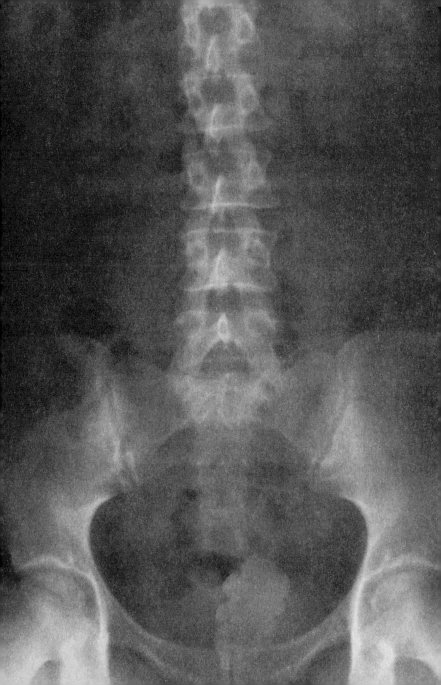

What Protects Us from the Protection?

It seems that every ER doctor at some point in his or her career encounters the case of having to retrieve the missing condom. While lubrication may add certain pleasure, it also causes condoms to slip off more easily. The moment of slippage is often not noticed, given that the users of the condom are focused on other sensations. Because of this oversight, the condom winds up forced farther into whatever crevice it may have dislodged.

Because retrieving a condom is not terribly difficult, no one should be dissuaded from using one. Using the same techniques that gynecologists use for a pelvic exam, a physician can insert a speculum to provide a better view of the area. With a simple light and pair of forceps the condom can be found, retrieved, and reused—okay, we're kidding about the last part.

A more dangerous situation than the lost and forgotten condom is the purposeful placement of condoms in the body to store illicit substances. The condoms can rupture, and the drugs, such as cocaine or heroin, are released into the body.

In general, though, the benefits of condoms far outweigh the risks. Like it says on the box, condoms can be more than 99 percent effective, *when used properly.*

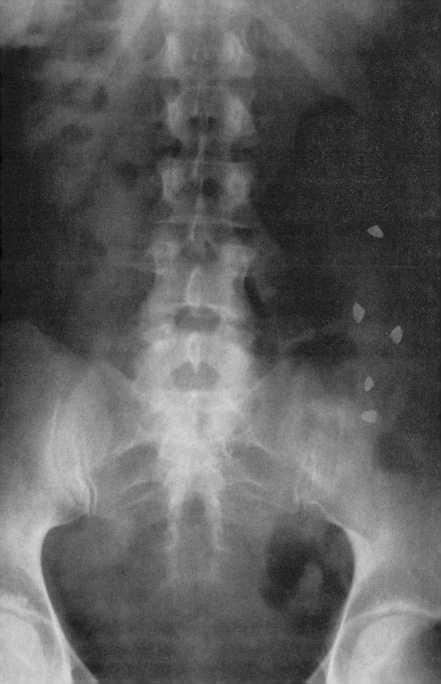

Give the Gift That Smells Forever

Diamonds have one of the hardest surfaces on earth, so why on earth would someone think to stuff them in an orifice?

For those who have ever had to save excessive amounts of money to buy an engagement ring or believe themselves to be socially enlightened because they saw the movie *Blood Diamond,* the answer is obvious. Diamonds are one of the most valuable substances on earth, no matter where they have been . . . although those mined from this location have got to be worth somewhat less.

As with anything that's valuable, there's an active smuggling industry. Many legitimate diamond retailers refuse to sell diamonds obtained through war or cruelty, dubbed *conflict diamonds.* As a result, many diamonds are smuggled in from these war-torn countries. Sometimes smugglers have to get creative as to where to hide these precious items; hence what we see in this X-ray.

Diamonds are called a girl's best friend, but we have a hard time imagining the girl who would want a diamond that was transported in this manner. Given such unknown origins and nontraditional transportation methods, one has to wonder if diamonds will continue to be used as engagement gifts.

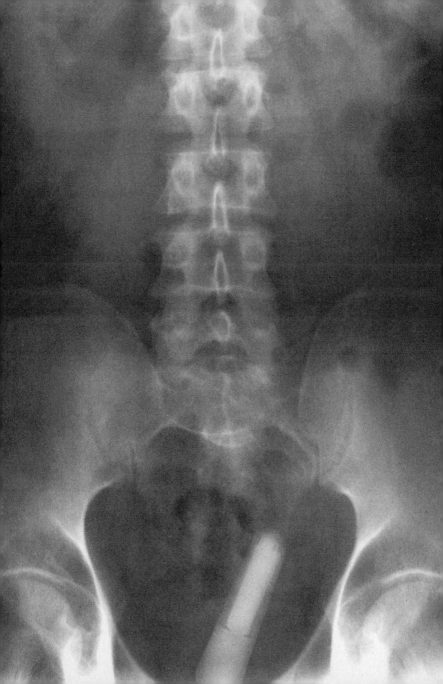

You Knew This Was Coming

We have way too many examples of stuck dildos—far, far more than we have room to include in this book.

Dildos are easier to retrieve than many of the other objects we've included in this book because their shape allows for both easy entry and exit, consistent with their intended use. Patients who use these objects most often require medical attention when the patients are engaging in this act by themselves. After penetration, patients cannot give themselves enough of a "reach-around" to retrieve and remove the object. Then, once alone and in this position, they find it difficult to call a friend at three in the morning and say, "Hey, could you do me a quick favor?"

Luckily for patients, when the bills go to the insurer, it just says, "foreign body removal." Otherwise, the insurer may wonder about some preexisting conditions.

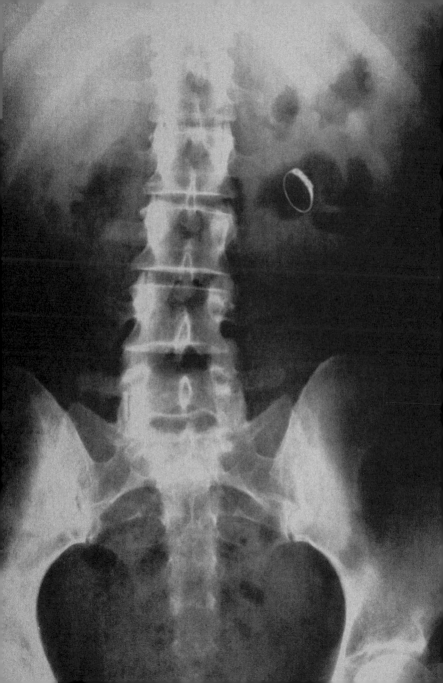

If You Like It, Then You Should Have Put a Ring In *It*

You have heard about men who propose by placing the engagement ring in the bottom of a champagne glass. Often, this creative method of proposal turns out well, but here is an example of when things go wrong.

This woman thought that waiting for her boyfriend to propose took forever. Well, she may be waiting just as long for this ring to pass. As we discuss throughout this book, the size and shape of an item will determine whether it travels through the gut and exits via the anus. Fortunately, her frugal boyfriend bought her a ring small enough to pass easily, which she surprisingly accepted and wore faithfully every day of her life.

The famous novelist Richard Bach has said, "True love stories never have endings." We disagree; this love story clearly began in the end.

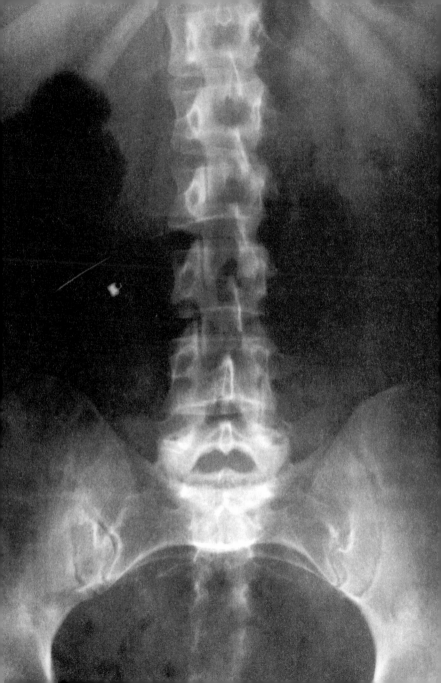

MEDICAL MALPRACTICE

Brush . . . Floss . . . Brush

Brace for this. Go figure that metal objects purposely put into the mouth *will* sometimes travel to the far side of the gastrointestinal system. This patient was just lucky he wasn't wearing headgear.

What most people don't appreciate is that often the bigger concern with braces is accidentally *inhaling* small parts of the braces, which can then end up in the lungs. Needless to say, if your lungs can't do their job, and you start turning blue due to the lack of oxygen, you are not going to look good, no matter how nice your smile is.

All joking aside, good oral health is important, not only so you can dazzle others with your pearly white, perfectly aligned, cavity-free teeth, but it can also be an indicator of overall general health. In fact, several studies have linked poor dental hygiene to an increased risk of heart disease and death. In other words, the benefits of proper oral care far outweigh the risk you see here.

So keep your braces on . . . but if you do happen to inhale, unlike a famous past president, just admit it, and get professional help.

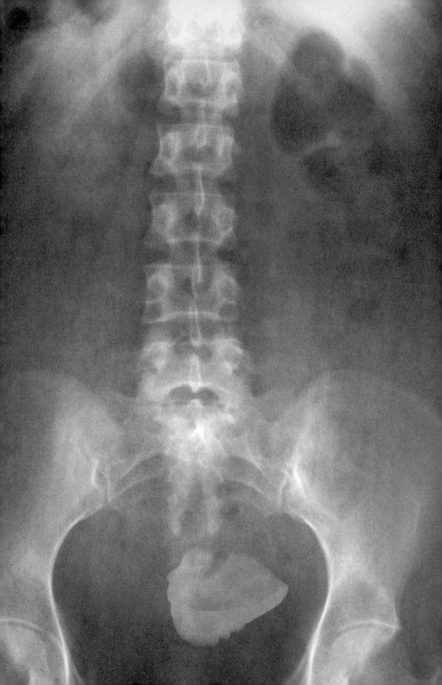

Chew on This

One of the authors once told a teacher he wanted to be a physician. The teacher, recognizing that offering some doubt might motivate the contrarian pupil further, replied, "Right now your head is so far up your ass if you bit down you'd get tonsillitis." Little did this teacher know that one day the student might grow up to write about teeth being able to achieve just that.

People are losing their dentures all the time, but usually not in this manner. Alas, not even Efferdent was enough to clean up this mess, though it might cause a nice, tingly feeling. Assuming that the patient would never want to put the dentures back in his mouth, the treating physician broke them into many pieces and removed the dentures piece by piece, or rather, tooth by tooth. Upon learning that he would have to buy a whole new set of dentures, the patient became upset and yelled, "You can bite my ass!"

When the dentist found out why the patient needed a replacement, he said, "Not again!" Apparently this person had a history of such behavior in the past. This is definitely *not* the reason why dentists want people to come back every six months!

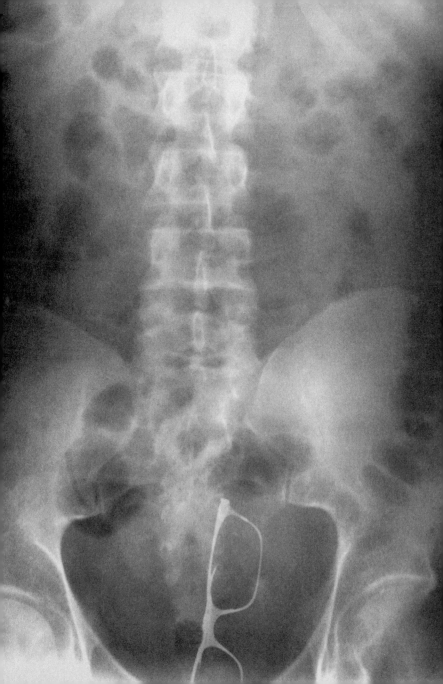

The Better to See What With?

"Honey, have you seen my glasses?" In this case, we don't think the patient would have found his glasses, even with the help of his glasses. These glasses were in serious trouble and would need more than a trip to LensCrafters.

As you may have guessed, the story given was that this patient was farsighted and not able to see the glasses right in front of him on the seat before he sat down on them. In fact, this patient was *very* farsighted and, because of this, required very thick lenses. While this arguably made the glasses dorky to wear, it also made them quite durable. So rather than shattering when the patient sat down on them, the glasses held together. Yet another reason to wear contacts.

The thick, curved glasses adjust the focus of light, re-adjusting the wearer's eyes to normal vision. This focusing of light is why eyeglasses can be used to focus the sun's rays on a small spot to cause intense heat. This patient didn't have to worry about such heat since his eyeglasses were, to use a beaten expression, where the sun didn't shine.

Ultimately, the patient was referred not only to his proctologist—Why did he already have one?—but also to a Lasik surgeon. We can imagine he might have said that he certainly learned his lesson from this incident, since having his glasses stuck up his buttocks gave him 20/20 (be?)hind-sight.

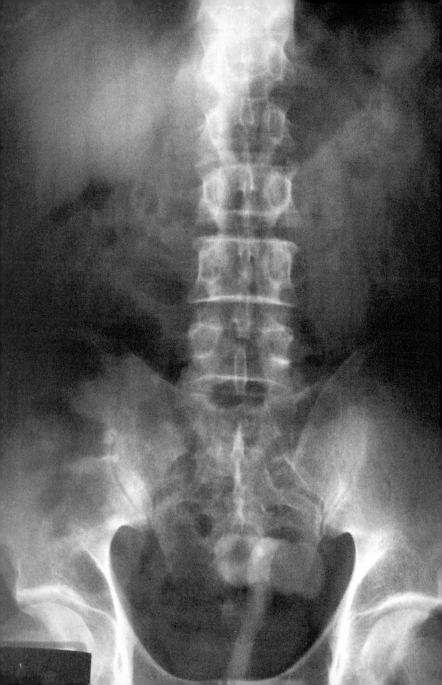

Order in the . . .

"Hear ye, hear ye." What was this gavel summoning? Hopefully better judgment and decision making in the future for this patient.

One might wonder if a person who places a gavel in his rectum would be "crazy." If someone who did this did, in fact, have a mental illness and was alleged to commit a crime, the law ensures that he must be competent to stand trial in order to be found guilty or innocent. While the specifics differ from state to state, finding someone incompetent to stand trial generally requires establishing that, as a result of a mental disease or defect, a person does not have a factual understanding of the legal proceedings and cannot work with an attorney.

Forensic psychiatrists are often called upon to give their opinions about a patient's competency to stand trial. Surgeons, on the other hand, are often called upon to remove the gavels. Given that the former involves examining above the eyebrows (i.e., brain/cognitive functioning), whereas the latter involves wiping the rear, we think it's obvious who has the better deal.

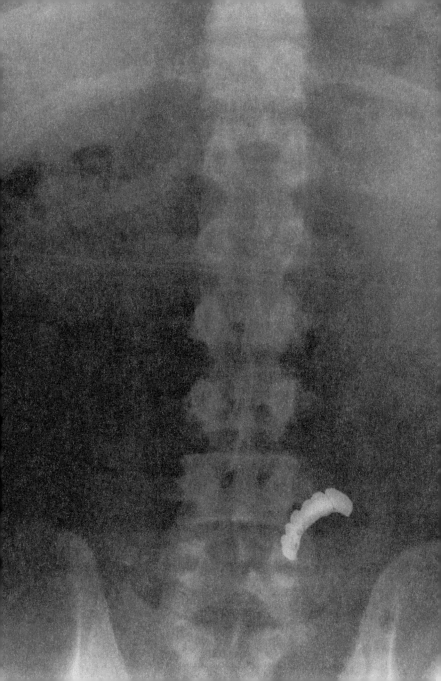

Bling, Bling!

Most people like to show off some on the outside, so what's wrong with showing off on the inside? A little strut for the gut if you will.

This wasn't for that purpose. We've seen cases in which people accidentally swallow dentures or braces, but in this case, the patient swallowed his *grill* (decorative mouth jewelry). This patient used to ask people, "Why you gotta be all up in my grill?" This was the first time anyone had the chance to ask him, "Why does your grill gotta be all up in you?"

We informed the patient that most likely the grill would just pass in his stool, and he could flush it away. He said that his grill was both personalized and costly enough that he did not want to lose it. He wanted to use it again.

At first, we were disgusted by his desire to use it again, but upon thinking about it, we understood. Although we all have a visceral reaction to putting in our mouth something that has been in excrement, with proper cleaning most objects can generally be sterilized of harmful bacteria. Compare this to our mouths, which, even after thorough cleanings and mouthwash, are consistently colonized with many types of bacteria. So now you know what people mean when they say, "You kiss your mother with that mouth?"

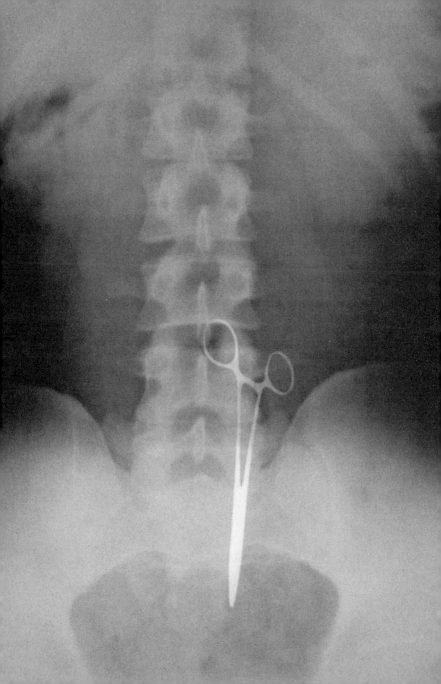

Clamping Arteries and Clipping Roaches

Invented by Drs. Jules-Émile Péan and William Halsted, a hemostat clamp is a scissorslike surgical instrument, usually used to control bleeding by clamping a blood vessel. Because hemostats are one of the most frequently used instruments, at times they are accidentally left in the bodies of patients. Fortunately, since they are usually made of surgical-grade steel, the hemostats are easily visible on X-ray imaging and can usually be removed without extreme difficulty, other than repeating the entire operation. This does often lead to pissing off a lot of people and exciting some lawyers.

The hemostat is also used for nonmedical purposes. For instance, many cannabis smokers use a hemostat as a "roach clip" to hold and smoke a stub of a marijuana cigarette, thus avoiding a burn on the fingers or mouth. While the inspiration for this ingenious use came more likely from Cheech and Chong than Drs. Péan and Halsted, at least no one has inhaled a hemostat . . . yet!

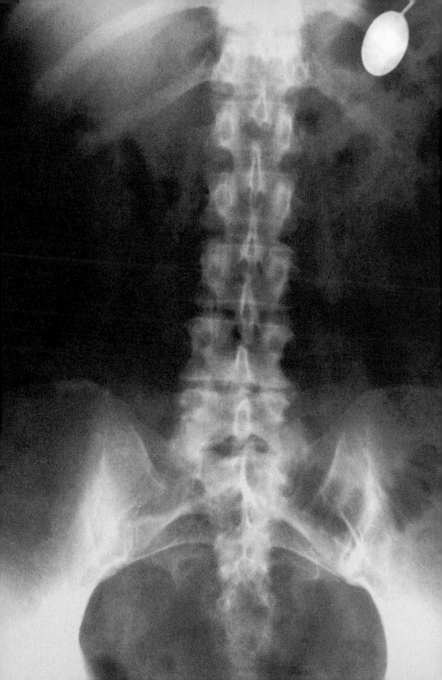

It Wasn't Any of Us

Many physicians prefer to carry their stethoscopes in a pocket, bag, in their hands, or simply not at all. However, the last place one would expect to find a stethoscope is inside the human body. We completely support the idea of listening to one's inner self, but we think this patient took it a bit too literally. But, alas, he is not alone.

One case of foreign bodies in the human body involved a young woman with a history of depression and a long-standing pattern of swallowing various objects in response to hearing voices that commanded her to do so. Over the course of fifteen years, she had at least seventeen surgeries at various hospitals to remove all of these objects. One of the more unusual objects she swallowed was the bell end of a stethoscope. For the physician in this case, it probably was one of the only times he listened to the stomach and had something listening back.

As for the stethoscope, it was safely removed, and it may be the only stethoscope that was ever placed *in* the intestines, rather than on them.

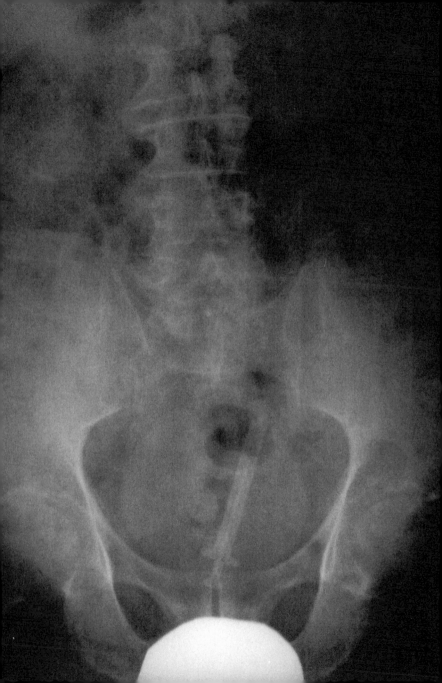

You're Giving Me a Shot Where?!

Many people have a fear of needles. Yet, as this patient demonstrates, syringes themselves don't scare people as much. People use syringes for various reasons, most legitimate, some not. We won't get into the "not."

The most common legitimate reason we see patients carrying syringes is for the treatment of insulin-dependent diabetes. The insulin isn't useful if it's swallowed because it's a type of protein, and proteins are broken down in the gut if taken by mouth. Injecting insulin is a way of bypassing this breakdown process. Although swallowing a syringe full of insulin doesn't make the insulin break down (the plastic syringe will protect it in the gut), the patient must have had a breakdown to actually do this.

It's very important to get insulin if we don't make it ourselves, and this patient understood the importance of getting insulin into the body, even if he did not completely understand the best method of delivery.

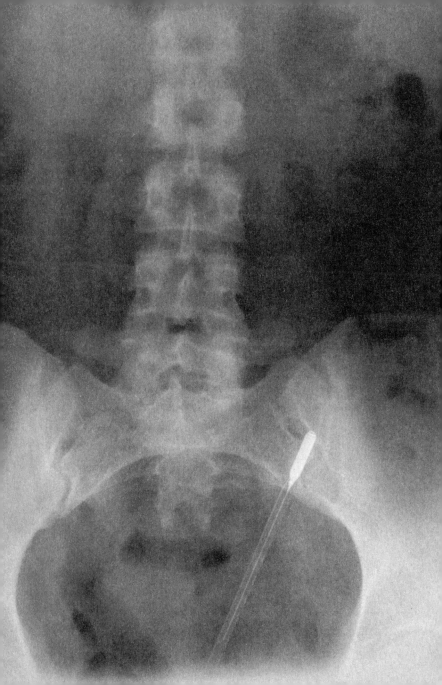

How Can You Distinguish an Oral Thermometer from a Rectal One?

By the taste of course! But seriously, if a mix-up does happen, a safer and definitely less gross way of distinguishing oral and rectal thermometers is by the color of the thermometer, and we don't mean the color brown.

This particular patient forgot one very important part of the instructions: After inserting the thermometer, whatever happens, *don't* let go of the other end!

Some of you may be wondering why rectal thermometers even exist, given that there are other traditional ways of measuring temperature, namely by mouth or in the armpit. Generally, rectal temperature reflects true core body temperature much more precisely than these other methods. More recently, measuring body temperature in the ear with an infrared thermometer has become the standard in most hospitals. Once again technology helps us escape certain pain-in-the-ass activities.

These new methods tend to be quite accurate, although far less suitable for this book.

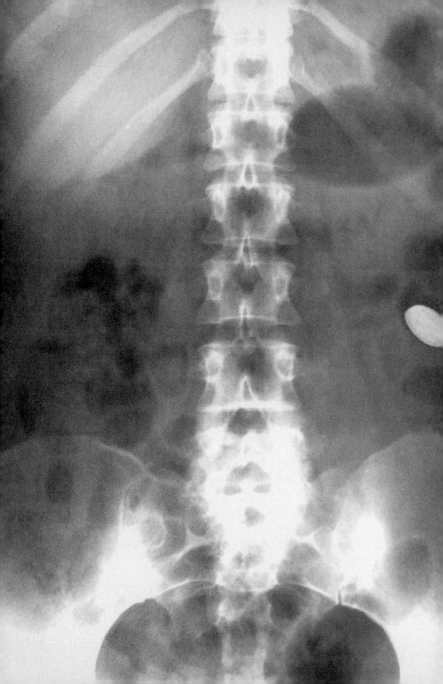

ODDS IN ENDS

No More Leakage

William Painter patented and developed the first leakproof bottle cap in 1892, although we doubt that he ever thought his brainchild would end up plugging a leak in someone's end. We can't help but wonder, does this make this bottle cap less collectible or more collectible?

Many of our readers may be familiar with another type of bottle cap: the candy with the same name. Bottle Caps, a Willy Wonka product, are chewable candies made in the flavors of various types of soda. The movie *Willy Wonka & the Chocolate Factory* gave us this candy as well as the beloved song "Pure Imagination," sung by Gene Wilder. We believe that many of the patients we have seen must love this song, as they clearly have an imagination. In fact, before we went into medicine we could never imagine people doing some of the things that we have seen. We are just waiting for the day when one of our patients can produce a golden ticket from down below. Hello, chocolate river!

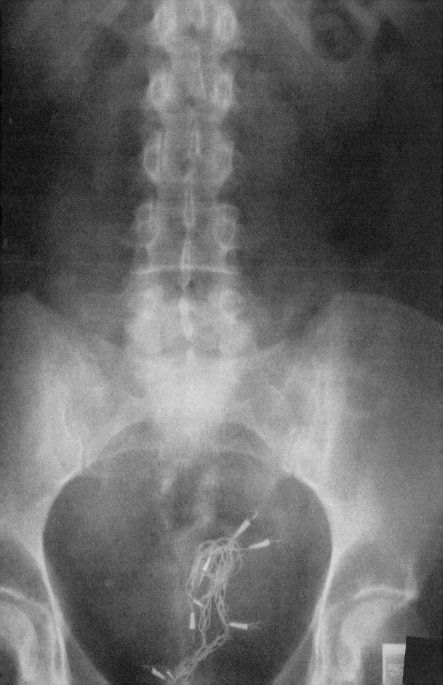

All Sorts of Things Happen at the
Office Christmas Party

Christmas lights come in all shapes, sizes, and, as this patient proves, can be used as decoration in all sorts of places.
One religious telling is that the lights on the tree are a re-
minder of the North Star that guided the three wise men to
the newborn baby Jesus. We wish there had been a wise
man to guide this patient away from the lights. Another version states that early Christians were persecuted for prac-
ticing their religion, so they would light trees to indicate
that a gathering was near. We found no traditional story
to explain this patient's particular use of lights.

Some Christmas lights are arranged in series, which is a
circuit through which electrical current flows in one line. If
a part of that circuit is broken or damaged, current can't
flow. So if one bulb is damaged, say from being cracked,
then the entire string does not light. In other words, this
patient should be careful not to squeeze or bear down if he
wants these lights to guide the way to his sacred place.

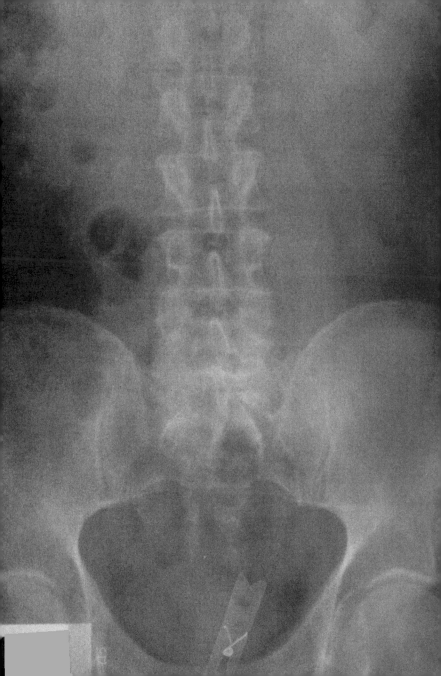

My Mother and Your Mother
Were Hanging Up Clothes

This children's counting rhyme continues with: "My mother punched your mother right in the nose. / What color was the blood?" Usually said among a group of children, the color is spelled out, and each color is counted per letter, leaving the last letter to be assigned to the child who is then designated as "It." In this case, the following rhyme may be more fitting: "My mother and your mother were acting real heinous. / My mother shoved a clothespin up your mother's . . ."

The clamping mechanism of the spring-drawn clothespin can induce some discomfort on the skin. If a clothespin were actually to clamp down on the intestine from the outside, as is occasionally necessary in surgery, an intestinal stricture could be created. Small intestinal strictures can be diagnosed by a small bowel follow-through exam, during which an X-ray is taken after the patient has swallowed liquid barium, which highlights the inner lining of the intestine that can then be viewed on X-ray. On the other hand, strictures in the large intestine, or colon, can only be viewed on X-ray after barium is inserted rectally. Finally, an appropriate case of rectal insertion.

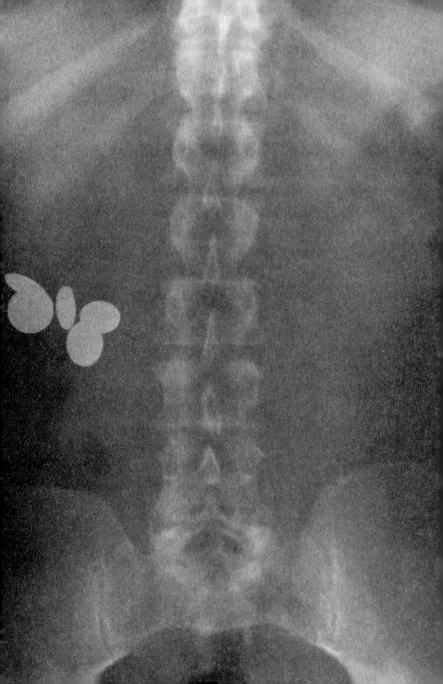

Keep the Change

Through these hard economic times, we are all trying to figure out the safest place to keep our money. We might consider real estate, stocks, bonds, a bank, or even under a mattress, but really, where else is safer than on ourselves, or rather inside ourselves, at all times?

Could this be why coins are the single-most commonly swallowed objects? Actually, this patient was not a saver; he was a smuggler. He swallowed rare coins in an attempt to transport them undetected. Unfortunately for him, metal detectors penetrate the skin.

As with any money—easy come, easy go. Almost all common coins will pass through the gastrointestinal tract without difficulty, with the exception of the occasional quarter or more uniquely shaped coin. Once a coin passes the narrowest point of the gastrointestinal tract—the area between your throat and your stomach—chances are nothing else will stand in its way.

Fortunately, most American coins are not likely to cause a chemical reaction inside the body. Since little harm comes with time, you have time to play the waiting game. Of course, if you are incredibly impatient to get your money, a little laxative can accelerate things right along and cause a run on the bank. This "fool and his money" were soon parted, and he no longer talked about loving the smell of money.

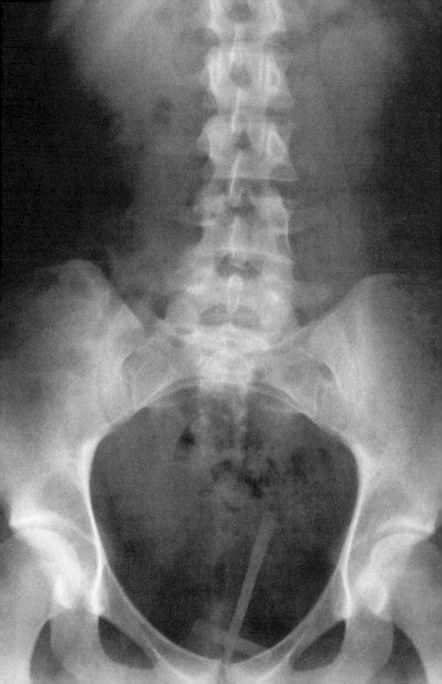

Crossing the Line

The idiom, "cross to bear," generally means having to carry a responsibility or burden. Tolstoy once said that although God sends a cross, God also sends the strength to bear it. While that may or may not be the case, God does not always provide guidance as to what to do with that cross.

For instance, a man with schizophrenia, who was in an inpatient psychiatric unit, deliberately ingested a crucifix after getting into a fight with another patient. Perhaps the patient should have just said some "Hail Marys." Sometimes, though, bearing a cross inside one's body requires a trip to purgatory better known as the operating room. One study examining thirty-six cases of foreign body ingestion revealed that four of the thirty-six objects were crucifixes. At least one of them required the patient to endure an operation because of a crucifix-induced blockage of what the patient ate.

We know that there are many people who believe that their bodies are temples and want to internalize God, but this goes a little too far. After all, does the Almighty really need to experience firsthand the half-digested burrito you had for dinner last night?

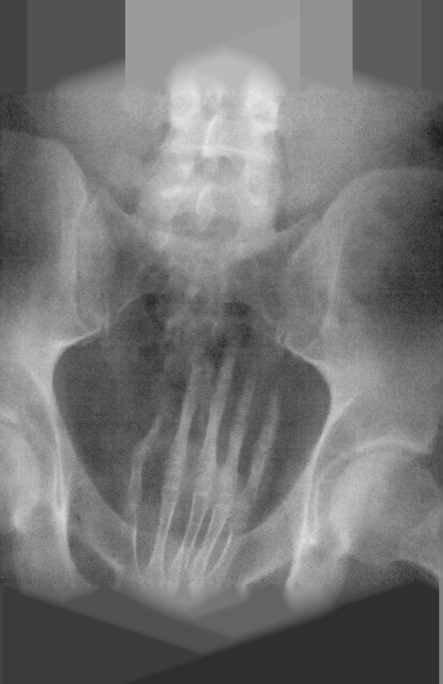

One Good Hand Deserves . . .

Yes, that's a hand. No, it does not belong there.

We admit that some people might find this amusing, and although it may bring some people great joy, it also represents our greatest fear. Physicians may have to perform manual disimpaction if a patient is severely constipated. A disimpaction requires the physician to use his hands to attempt to break up any hard, dry, and impacted stool in the rectum. (Please keep this in mind next time you hear someone complain about doctors making too much money.) This procedure actually isn't very easy, and the doctor needs to be pretty aggressive. We've always feared that if we are too aggressive we could wind up in this situation pictured here. When a doctor gets stuck, who is supposed to fix that?

Although the patient tried to play this situation off casually, ultimately he admitted to the truth. He played the finger game with someone else, another practice that we do not recommend. The finger game involves a person trying to see how much of their hand they can fit inside someone else, starting with one finger and going from there. We are guessing these two people are the world champions.

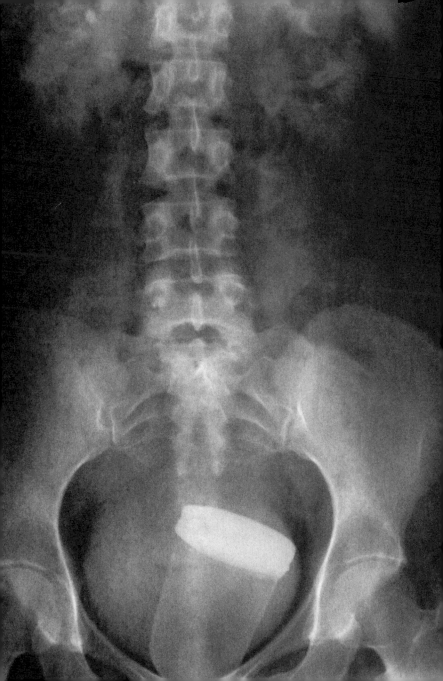

When Is a Rectum Not Closed? When It Is A-Jar!

We've seen bottles, we've seen cups, we've seen about every receptacle that you can imagine go into this receptacle. This clever person realized that you can house almost anything in your rectum using the same device people have used for centuries to store nearly anything anywhere. With a plain old jar, one can preserve anything . . . even preserves!

The question then becomes what to store in the jar. What do you really want to preserve or not want to lose?

In this case, the patient was not actually trying to get something in; he was trying to get something out. The story he told us was that he could not for the life of him open a small jar of pickles. He just didn't have a strong enough grip. He thought long and hard about how he could get a tighter grip on the lid. Eventually he discovered the location of the tightest grip in his body, and he attempted to use it to his advantage. Unfortunately, his hand grip was so weak by then that he lost hold of the object. The rest is history.

The patient admitted that the inspiration was not completely his own. He got the idea from other people who often referred to him as a tight-ass.

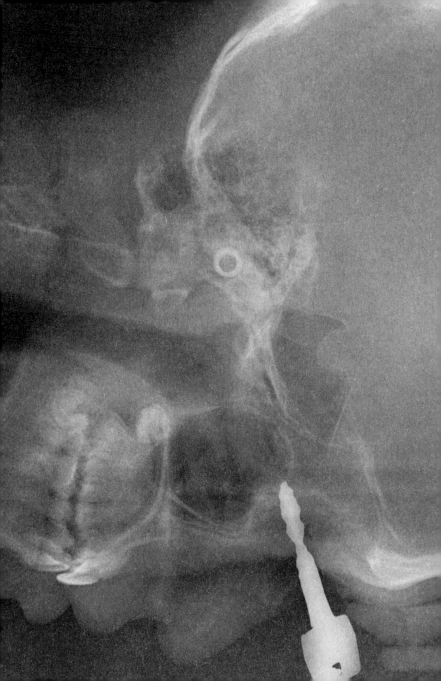

They Are Always in the Last Place You Look

Have you ever misplaced your glasses, only to find them on your head already?

This patient came to the emergency room thinking he was psychotic until he found out the truth. Several days prior he could not find his keys, yet he complained of hearing his keys everywhere he moved. He swore he could also smell and taste them, but he just could not find them.

He began asking everyone he knew if they had seen his keys. He explained that each time he asked a person, that person would look at him as if he were crazy and always replied, "They are right in front of your face." He started to believe everyone around him was executing a massive conspiracy against him.

The X-ray (we're avoiding any "skeleton key" jokes) ultimately helped the patient realize deep down what he already suspected might be going on. The "key" for this patient was recognizing that there were many things he wasn't seeing in addition to his keys, including the penetrating injury to his own eye. Eye penetrations are diagnosed by placing a fluorescent dye over the eyeball and then shining a special blue light on the eye. If any fluorescent fluid, or "aqueous humor," is found leaking out of the eye, this means the eyeball has been penetrated . . . a situation completely devoid of any humor whatsoever.

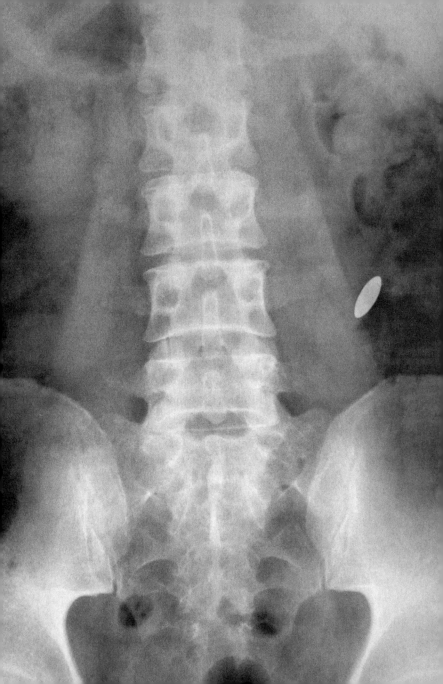

A Penny, No Matter Where It Is Saved, Is a Penny Earned

Benjamin Franklin is credited with a slight different variation of the above saying. We think he'd agree that there are much, much better places to save one's pennies than the location used by this patient. For one, there is the obvious drawback of having to run to the toilet instead of the ATM when correct change is needed. We know ATM fees are high, but come on!

Incidentally, the first U.S. penny was made of 100 percent copper. Since 1982, the penny has been made of 97.5 percent zinc and 2.5 percent copper. Although these trace elements are essential for a healthy body, swallowing or licking pennies is *not* a good way to obtain the daily recommended allowance of these minerals. In fact, there are documented cases of zinc toxicity due to the swallowing of pennies, and at least one case of death after chronic ingestion of 425 pennies, equivalent to the median price of a home in Detroit.

One can get copper toxicity, too, but typically not from depositing pennies in the rectal vault. Although that may be good news for the patient, the poor penny is screwed either way. Interestingly, the metal value of a copper penny is 2.44 cents, giving you an instant 144 percent return on your investment. Forget about penny stocks, just focus on the pennies!

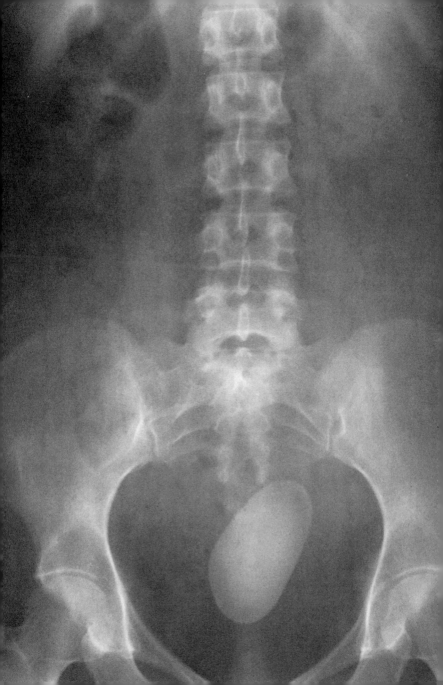

THE NOT-SO-GREAT OUTDOORS

Not Everybody Must Get Stoned

The term, "*cobble*," derived from the British word, *cob*, for "rounded lump," with *cobble* then meaning "little rounded lump." In this case, real cobblestones were found in this patient, instead of the usual rounded lumps one might find.

In the seventeenth century the British took their fondness for even larger stones, or rather boulders, and applied it to the legal field. When a defendant refused to speak, he was brought to a dungeon, placed on the ground with arms and legs spread apart, and tied to posts. A sharp boulder was then placed beneath his back, while boulders and rocks were piled onto the defendant's chest until he spoke. Nonetheless, many people still believe that the placement "on" is better than *in*.

In today's legal system when a defendant's sanity is questioned, for the purpose of being tried in court, modern proceedings call for a forensic psychiatrist to do a "Competency to Stand Trial" evaluation. If a defendant claims that he is not competent to stand trial because, for instance, he has stones in his rectum, he will find that this is not a sound argument. Although probably uncomfortable, having a stone lodged in the colon has no bearing on one's understanding of legal proceedings or overall ability to work with counsel. The defendant would find himself between a rock and a hard place.

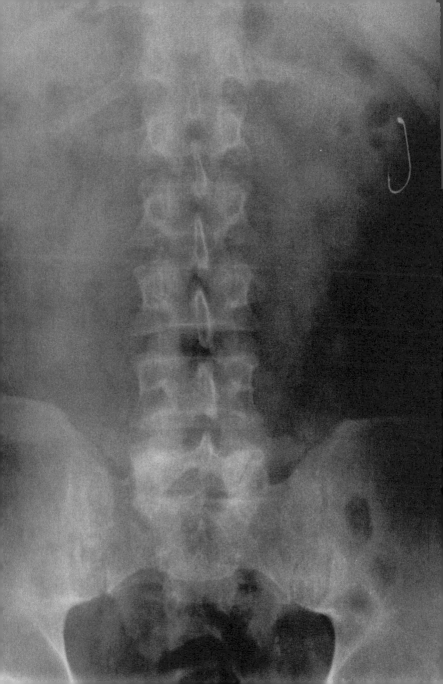

Swallowing Hook, Line, but at Least Not the Sinker

Lao Tzu, the ancient Taoist sage, purportedly said, "Give a man a fish and you feed him for a day. Teach a man to fish, and you feed him for a lifetime." Sounds great . . . except in our litigious society, you better include a disclaimer waiving responsibility if the recipient accidentally swallows or gets impaled by the fishhook. Admittedly, accidental ingestion of fishhooks in human beings is far rarer than accidental fishhook stabbings. We do know of one woman who presented to the ER complaining of belly pain. An X-ray and a CT scan, followed by surgery, revealed a fishhook connected to a small piece of fishing line. We assume that she must have been cut loose after she was caught.

There are many ways to remove fishhooks. A physician can numb the area and potentially dig the hook out with forceps. Alternative methods include taking wire cutters to cut off the tip. One can also try to pull the hook back through the path of the skin; this method requires the use of a string or one's hand to guide the tip during removal so that it does not get caught.

So if you do find yourself hooked, or you have hooked someone else, just make sure to drag yourself or pull them to your nearest emergency department. Or alternatively, a hardware store, if you want to take a risk and save on your co-pay.

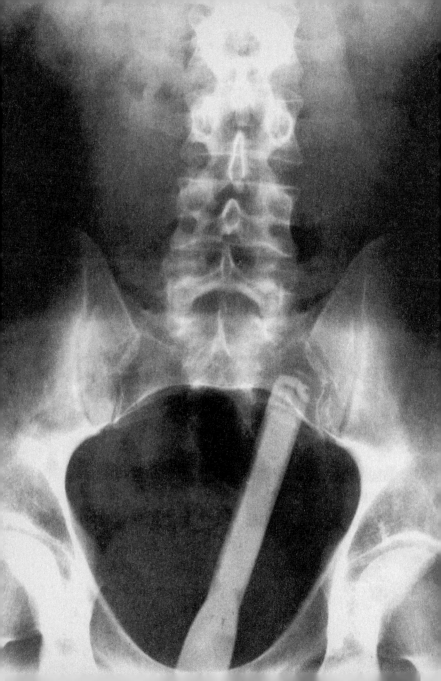

Let There Be Light!

In its 100-plus-year history, the flashlight has been used to light many dark recesses, as in this case.

When one of the authors was a boy scout twenty years ago he hated those ten-mile hikes lugging his heavy gear, including his large flashlight. If only the flashlights could be made smaller. Well, it looks like they were.

The name "flashlight" is based on the fact that early flashlight bulbs and batteries were not efficient enough to sustain long-lasting light and could only produce brief flashes or pulses of light. We imagine these brief pulses and flashes are still much more light than this patient would want us to shed on his case.

Inserting a flashlight in the rectum offers "advantages," ranging from sheer exploration to, if feeling especially daring and creative, holding the light by one "end" and making shadow puppets. However, if the flashlight gets stuck, you need to hike bent over and walk backward.

In addition to the corrosive effects of the batteries, there is also the possibility of electric shocks from the battery—not the kind of stimulation most people have in mind when they perform this action. Although this tempts us to recommend using solar-powered flashlights instead (not a joke, they do exist), is there really a point to sticking it where the sun don't shine?

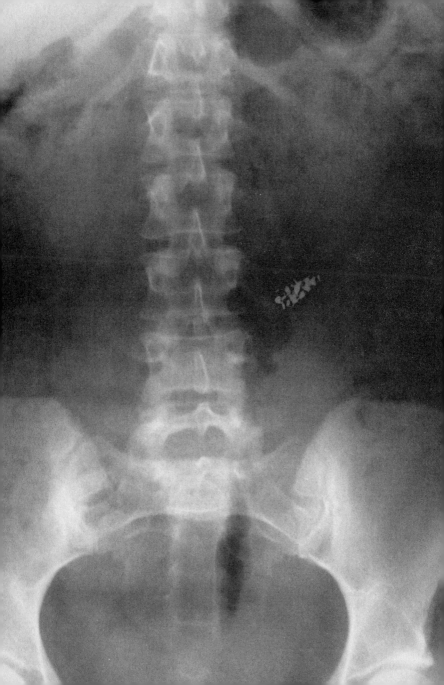

Something to Fill in the Hole

Yes, this is a stomach filled with gravel. No, this person, a bodybuilder, was not the product of hazing or forced to eat gravel by neighborhood bullies. Nor did he do it because he thought his "abs of steel" should be accompanied by "guts of concrete." This person actually suffered from a condition known as *pica*. This disorder is described as an uncontrollable desire to eat nonnutritious foods, including gravel, dirt, chalk, soap, and, some might add, McDonald's.

Pica has been thought to be associated with a nutritional deficiency, most commonly iron deficiency. Recent research suggests that this disorder is tied to obsessive-compulsive disorder, or OCD, and schizophrenia. In general, most people eat more when stressed, but individuals with pica take stress-induced eating to a new level. Treatment consists of fixing the cause, whether it is a nutritional or psychological deficiency, or at least trying to crush up Oreo cookies so they look like dirt.

Interestingly, pica appears to have a cultural and pregnancy-related component. In fact, according to a study published in 2004, the prevalence of pica during pregnancy is "between 8% and 65%." Who can blame them, though? After all, they are eating dirt for two.

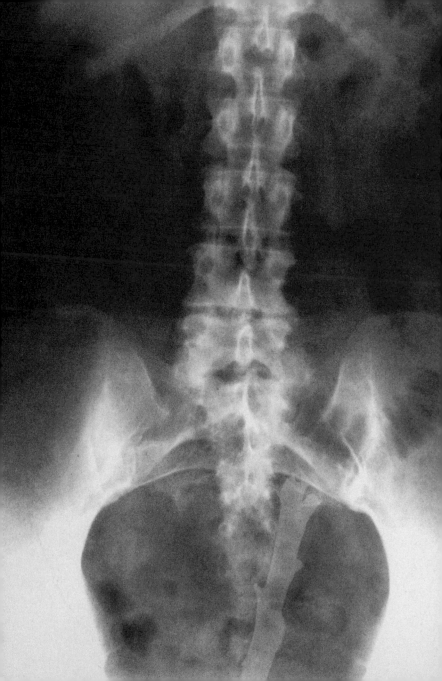

A Stuck Stick

We all know individuals who seem to have a stick up the ass. Such actual impalement can be serious. For instance, in the case of one adult man who presented to the ER with a stick in his bottom, the patient reported that two men had robbed him and then shoved the stick inside him. Basically, the patient got a stick up after a stick-up.

Because the stick was too high to be removed nonsurgically, he required a laparotomy, or surgical opening of the abdomen, and the stick was "milked" downward and delivered via the rectum, much like a baby would be delivered. And women often say men can never know what that's like.

Later, as patients often do, he admitted that he had actually inserted the stick himself. The truth, and literally the stick, came out in the end.

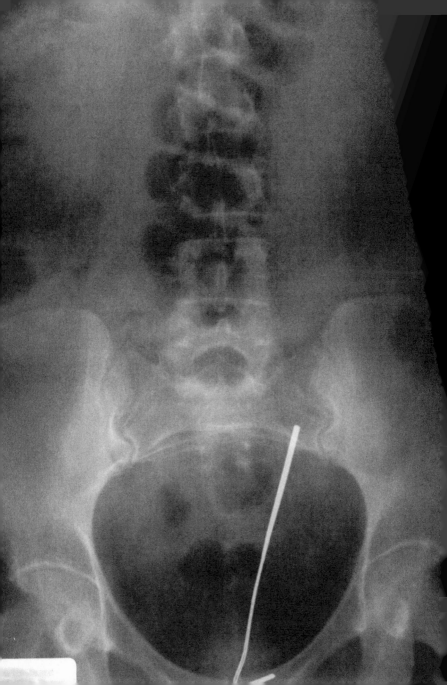

Talk About High

Camping is a leisurely activity for some and a dreaded annual event for others. This person found a unique way to enjoy his camping trip.

One of the more challenging aspects of a weekend camping in the mountains can be the altitude. Very high altitude is considered to be 11,500 feet to 18,050 feet. This is the most common range for severe altitude sickness, which can consist of headache, dizziness, poor sleep, nausea, decreased exercise tolerance, dehydration, and, to put it mildly, altered thinking.

This sort of mental sickness can happen regardless of how intelligent you are. A physician we knew once told us that during a hiking trip he suddenly removed all of his clothing. We wonder if he suffered the same fate as the person who ended up with the tent stake in the wrong place.

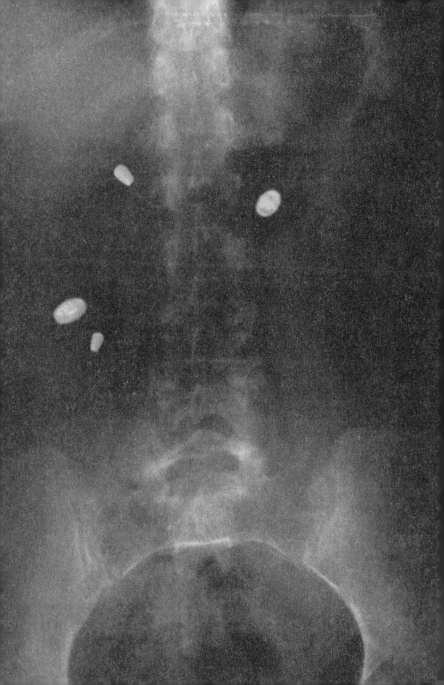

This Kid Was Hooked

We've described a few cases of lead poisoning from in-dwelling foreign bodies, but we always seem to find more.

This patient, an eight-year-old boy, had a history of attention deficit/hyperactivity disorder (ADHD), coupled with a learning disability, and pica. The patient had X-ray films taken, which revealed multiple lead fishing sinkers in his small and large intestines. As you can see, lead-based objects are quite visible on X-ray images because they block the ray beam. This blockage explains why Superman could not see through lead and why we wear lead-plated underwear.

Although they can cause serious problems inside the body, lead-based sinkers pose a much greater threat to fish and birds. Marvin Gaye sang about "fish full of mercury" in "Mercy Mercy Me" in 1971, yet the danger of fish and birds full of lead is still very real today. And for those that don't care much about the environment and only about humans, such toxicity in turn poses a threat to humans who might consume these fish and birds. Perhaps instead of selling organic fish and poultry we should just be given the choice of leaded or unleaded.

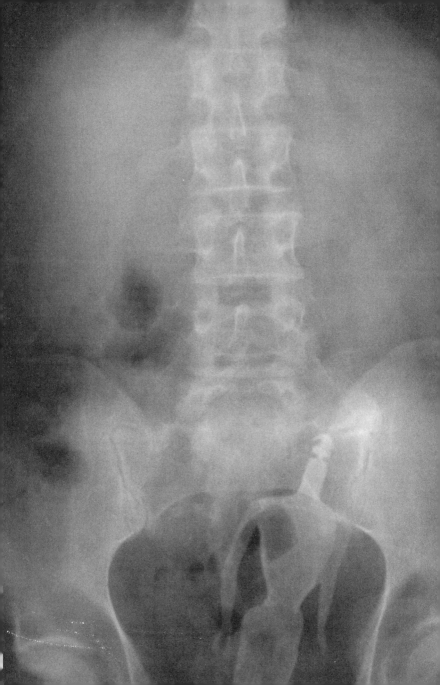

TOYS IN TROUBLE

I'm a Barbie Girl, in a Where?

"I was taken out of my Malibu Dream House for this?" Poor Barbie. We sincerely sympathize with her situation. Where was Ken when Barbie suffered this indignity, or do we not want to know? You have to wonder, though, couldn't the designer of Barbie have anticipated this?

In a BBC News report, Barbie's physical dimensions were applied to a real woman who was five feet six inches tall and had a twenty-eight-inch waist. If the woman's height were to remain unchanged, her waist would have to be twenty inches, her bust would be twenty-seven inches, and her hips twenty-nine inches to match Barbie's proportions. The closest examples of such body types that we found were on the *The Real Housewives of Orange County*, although most people we know recognize that none of these shapes come naturally. Many, therefore, argue that this shape gives women a wholly unrealistic expectation of what their own bodies should look like and encourages women to undergo risky surgeries.

The doll's long, thin shape does lead to other possible uses, though. In other words, another argument for making the Barbie figure more realistic (i.e., similar to the typical female body) is that if it were reflective of the average human being's dimensions, this situation may have never occurred!

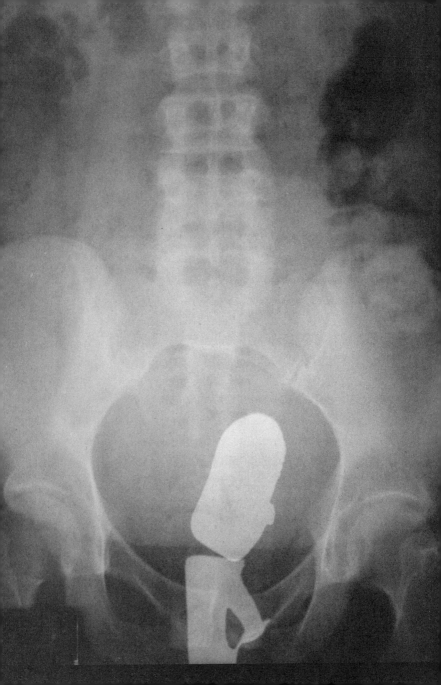

Don't Put Yourself in These Shoes

Parents try to capture the fleeting moments of youth in many ways. They videotape, audio tape, make handprints, keep baby clothing, and occasionally bronze baby shoes to create mementos of those early, precious days of life. It becomes unbearable for some as their progeny learn to drive, go off to the senior prom, and eventually to college. Some mothers and fathers just cannot let go . . . this patient was one of them. Of course, it might have been easier to let go if this patient were not so tight-assed.

These symbols of innocence, used here for not such an innocent purpose, may be more regularly required around the time when a child learns to walk. Pediatricians often tell parents that they can expect a child to start walking around twelve months of age, although the normal age range during which a child may walk is between nine and eighteen months old. Many parents think if their child is ahead of the curve early in life, that will be true for the rest of his or her life, but research does not necessarily support this claim. Anecdotally, one of the authors of this book didn't speak a word until he was almost four years old, and now he won't shut up.

So let the shoes be a fond memento, rather than a demonstration of strict parenting, or anal retentiveness, so to speak. And you thought your shoes stink.

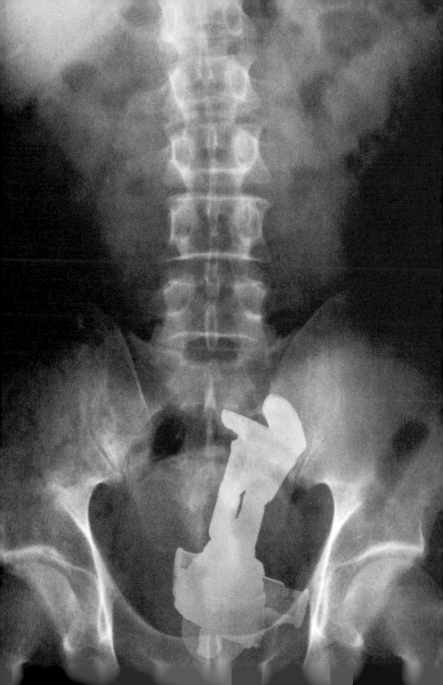

To Infinity and Beyond

Buzz Lightyear typically isn't found without his companion Woody, though we are glad Woody wasn't found here. Otherwise we'd have to talk about how the patient had a woody stuffed up his bottom.

The wild adventures of Woody and Buzz have brought them to the harrowing jaws of a giant toy claw, the hands of the nefarious toy-terrorizer Sid Phillips, the clutches of the sociopathic teddy bear Lotso, and a few canine confrontations as well. It appears none of his enemies chose to follow him here, as this is a far more harrowing adventure than any Buzz has seen before.

Between 1995–99, China's Thinkway Toys produced a talking Buzz Lightyear action figure that spoke phrases voiced by the original Buzz Lightyear, Tim Allen. We're sure poor Buzz would have cried for help here, but sadly in this space, just like in outer space, no one can hear his screams.

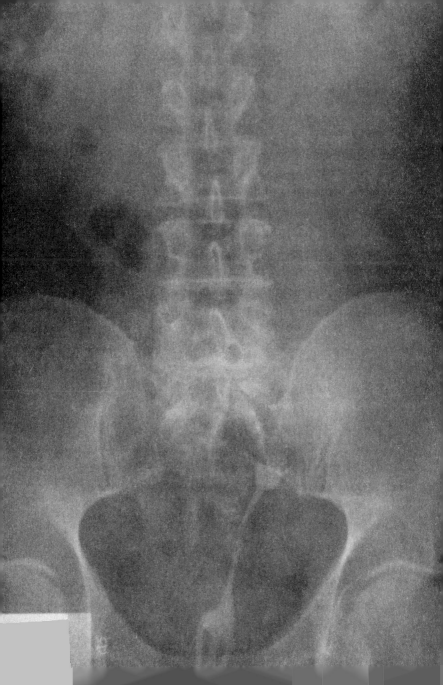

All the Way from Mada-gas-canal

The giraffe is a magnificent animal in many ways. It's the tallest land-living animal—sorry Shaq—as well as the largest ruminant, an animal that rechews its food after the food has been in the stomach (one of us has a regurgitating baby niece who does something disturbingly similar). Fortunately, the giraffe doesn't do the same thing to food at the other end. Needless to say, the most distinct feature about the giraffe is its long neck, which is used in feeding, combat, and, when it comes to toy versions, some other rather "unusual" behavior that would have made Geoffrey the Giraffe and the entire Toys "R" Us Giraffe family blush. Perhaps this practice is what gave this toy giraffe its brown spots?

Old giraffe males are called *stink bulls* due to their hair naturally containing antibiotics and parasite repellants. We imagine the same name can be given to the poor toy giraffes that have had the misfortune of being inserted up the "gas canals" of the patients we and our colleagues have seen. We hope the giraffe is careful, as it's a zoo in there!

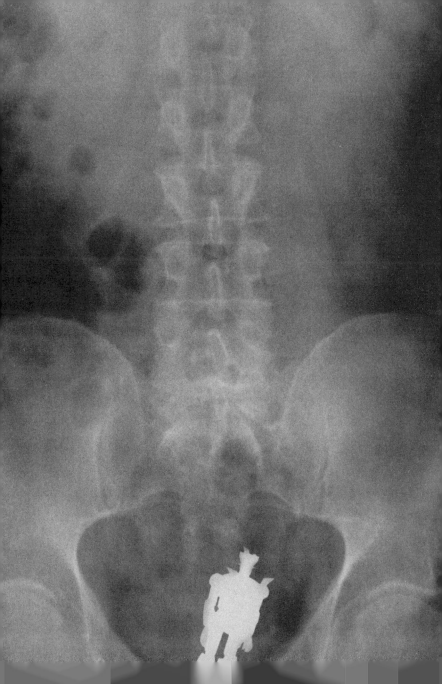

More Than Meets the Eye

What was the patient hoping this would transform to? We don't know, but much like Obama so far for some people, it didn't lead to the change the patient was hoping for.

Interestingly, Transformers were predated by GoBots, which had similar vehicular-robotic metamorphoses. However, GoBots figures were not as successful as Transformers, possibly due to the lack of detail in the transformation of GoBots, which had rigid straight extremities as opposed to the flexibility of Transformers. This is likely why Transformers are apparently also more popular for this activity.

The rigid, straight extremities of GoBots actually simulate a very serious medical condition that can occur in human beings after brain damage. Extremities can become quite rigid and extended at a person's sides. This posturing is often an ominous sign, reflecting not only the shape of the GoBots but their poor outcome as well. At least the GoBots escaped this Transformer's ordeal, lending credence to the belief that some fates are worse than death. In fact the only way this Transformer is going to make it back to Cybertron is if this dude eats some serious FiberCon.

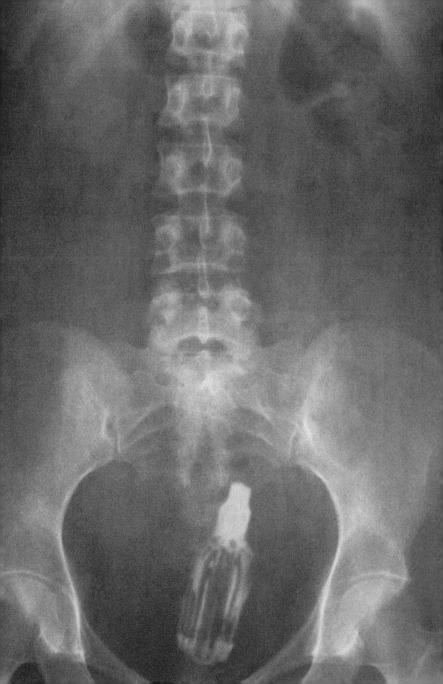

WAY TOO PERSONAL FOR HYGIENE

Perhaps the Best Place to Use It

Advertisements for body sprays often imply that women find men who use body spray utterly irresistible. Television commercials have shown that men who use body spray are able to place women under spells, which make them unable to keep their hands off the highly aromatic male bodies. Somehow, we do not think this use of body spray would create the same effect.

Perhaps this particular patient practiced the age-old pastime of "fart burning" and sought to add a more explosive effect to his talent. While we are not aware of scientific studies documenting the flammability of flatulence, gases that are the byproduct of bacterial digestion in the gastrointestinal system are, in fact, combustible. These gases include methane, carbon dioxide, hydrogen, and hydrogen sulfide. This patient may have believed that with the added alcoholic content of a body spray, the pyrotechnics he could emit would be awe-inspiring.

The surgeons who removed this can were truly awed, although more by the patient's dim wits than his bright flatus.

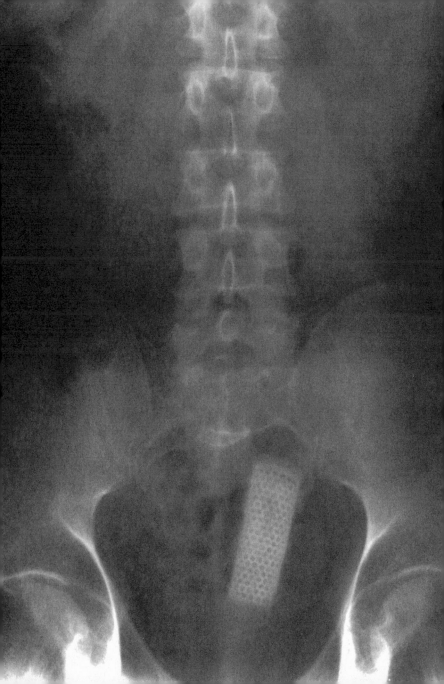

If Down There Doesn't Look Good, We Don't Look Good

We were at first surprised to find this hair care product in an area without a lot of hair, or at least where hair is only on the outside (in some more than others). Ultimately, though, the structure of the brush explained its alternative use. Notice we say, "explained," and not "justified."

A curling brush, with its brush prongs arranged in a 360-degree pattern, provides an ideal shape to maximize tactile stimulation of the area one is brushing. The curling brush's shape also makes it "form-fitting" for placement anywhere. Commercial pet brushers always mention both the ability to brush fur and "give your pet a massage" because the numerous contacts designed to get the most amount of fur also increase the sensation of touch. We do not endorse this alternative brush use for yourself or your pet.

We recommend limiting your curling to the hair on your head only. If you find that your curling brush is just too tempting, get a perm.

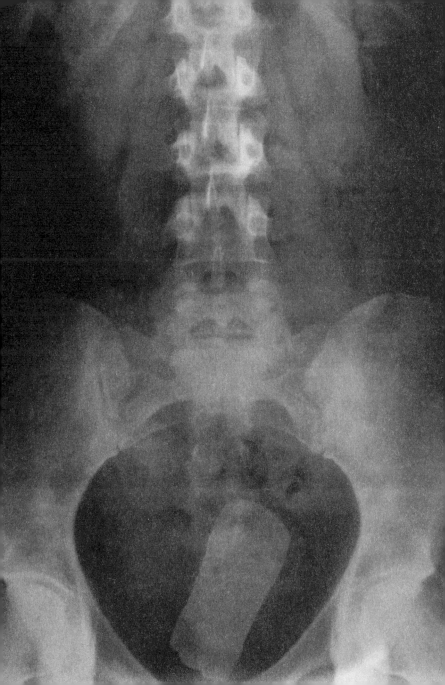

If You Have to Put Up Something,
This Is Probably the Best Choice

An individual walks into a pharmacy and asks for deodorant for their butt. When the pharmacist says that such a thing does not exist, the customer claims that he bought it before and hands the pharmacist the empty container. Upon examining it, the pharmacist remarks that it's an empty container of normal underarm deodorant. At this point, the customer gets annoyed, snatches the container back from the pharmacist, and reads out loud the directions: TO APPLY, PUSH UP BOTTOM.

While this misunderstanding may be the stuff of jokes, there are certainly similar documented cases. In one case, doctors removed a can of deodorant spray from a patient's rectum and made a video of the procedure, showing doctors and nurses joking and laughing. The video was posted on the Internet, which resulted in the patient getting upset and an investigation into the conduct of the medical professionals, with subsequent charges against some individuals. Hence, the reason this book is not a TV show.

In another case, a patient had a deodorant can up his rectum that caused the rectal skin to become trapped in the bottle, requiring an operation. The surgeons were at least appreciative of the choice of object. And you thought your farts smelled like roses.

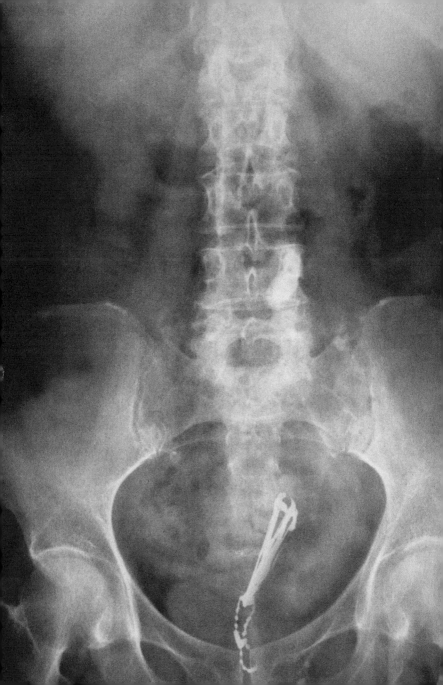

Nailed It

The styles of nail clippers vary widely. Most people are familiar, apparently sometimes intimately, with the type of clipper shown in this X-ray. The patient here said that since he did not have his nail clipper, he figured he would wait until his nails were long enough to reach it. The world record for the longest nails, by the way, is about thirty-six inches, or about three feet. With nails this long, one can reach many more things than one would otherwise be able to without the Freddy Krueger fingers.

In addition to extending people's reach, nails can also act as a clue for physicians. Some illnesses are accompanied by characteristic nail changes and can aid physicians in making a diagnosis. For example, when someone is poisoned with arsenic, horizontal lines, usually white in color and called Mees' lines, develop along the nails of fingers and toes. Damaged nails may also reveal dysfunction in other organs, such as the liver, kidney, or thyroid. If someone has a change in color, shape, or texture of the nail, fungus or bacteria may also be a possible culprit.

In this individual's case, cutting his nails with this particular clipper, once retrieved, will undoubtedly affect both the appearance and odor of the nails.

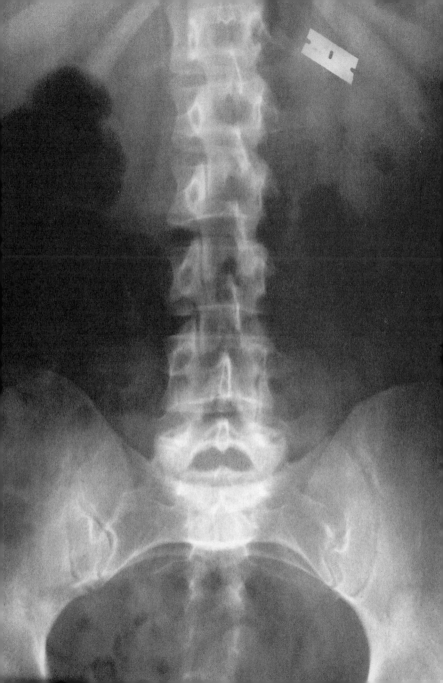

The Best a Man Can Ingest

You would assume a razor blade would be the last thing someone would swallow. Based on our experience, we've learned not to assume anything because we have seen people who will consume everything.

For example, one study describes 101 foreign body ingestions, 8 of which were razor blades. Surprisingly, in this study, none of the perforations resulted from razor blades, with more common causes of perforations being from toothpicks and animal bones.

In another series of case reports, a thirty-one-year-old man with various psychiatric diagnoses was witnessed swallowing razor blades. The patient reported having done this forty times, as he felt this helped relieve his stress. We, on the other hand, just exercise or eat some ice cream when feeling stressed out.

Safety razors have evolved much, with modern versions incorporating as many as five blades per disposable cartridge. Because their annual cost approaches close to what a solid gold razor would cost, a large number of men worldwide continue to use the traditional double-edge blades, which cost as little as 10 cents per blade. The double-edge blades also pose less risk upon swallowing, although you could argue the five-blade razors go down "smoother."

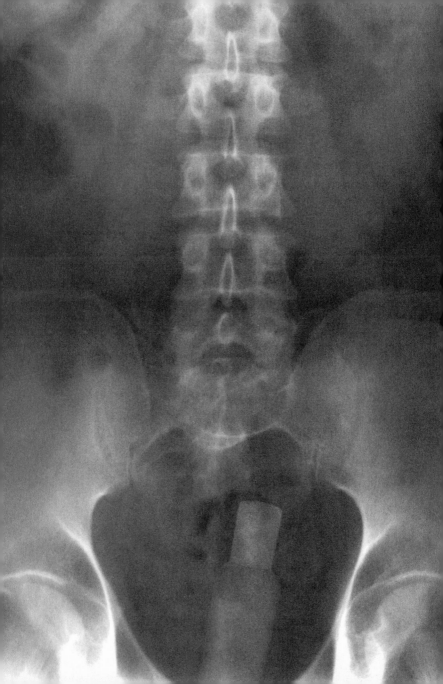

To Poo or Not to Poo

Now, you would think that a product designed for the head would not accidentally end up in the other end, seeing how they are located relatively far from each other, except for those individuals who have their heads up their asses. But as you can see in the X-ray, it does happen. We realize that the gut has lots of folds and probably is not easy to manage, but it's best to leave the shampoo for managing just hair.

A major concern about having shampoo inside one's bowels, aside from walking funny, is the potential toxicity resulting from the shampoo if the bottle were to leak. For instance, a study published in a medical journal found that infants had detectable levels of certain toxic substances due to being exposed to shampoos. Some of these substances can affect human male development and may have other harmful effects yet unknown. Therefore, it may be advisable to keep certain substances in some shampoos out of one's hair, and certainly nowhere near one's genitalia.

In fact, many people have started boycotting all shampoos, adopting the "No 'Poo Movement," or only using shampoos made from natural ingredients like vinegar, olive oil, and so on. Ironically, this patient had a shampoo bottle inside him, and because of that, had no poo at the same time.

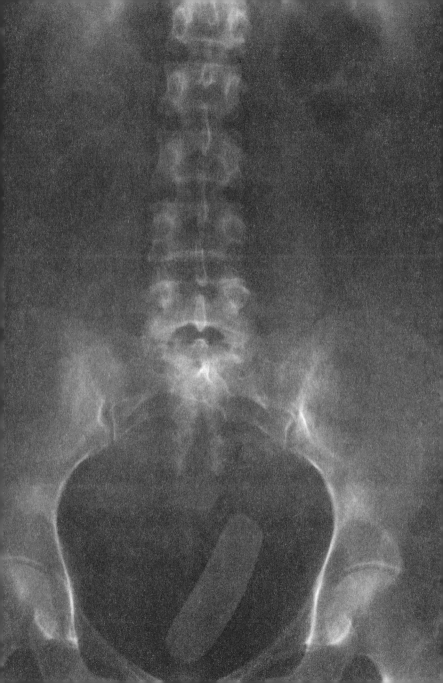

Is This Why You Shouldn't Bend
Over to Pick Up Soap in the Shower?

Soap has a lot of great features for many possible uses, including some unorthodox ones. (See attached image.) One can adjust the shape and size of a bar of soap to fit any nook or cranny. Soap is self-cleaning; so no matter where it goes, it's still ready for use anywhere else. However, we recommend giving the soap at least a quick rinse if found in this location.

It turns out this patient merely practiced good hygiene, or so he said. As the soap whittled down in size, it accidentally slipped inside when the patient was cleaning below.

Soap is slippery because of its chemical properties. The molecules of soap have water-loving heads and oil-loving tails. Since oil and water do not mix, the oils get dispersed, making soap a great cleaning agent. Plus, by combining the slipperiness of oil and water in a wet bar of soap, you get an object so slippery when wet that Bon Jovi named an album after it. At least, we assume it was just soap he was referring to. This slipperiness also makes wet soap a great lubricant, although we figure that had no relevance here.

Ultimately, the patient felt very guilty about what happened. We thought that he had already punished himself enough, having already washed himself out with soap.

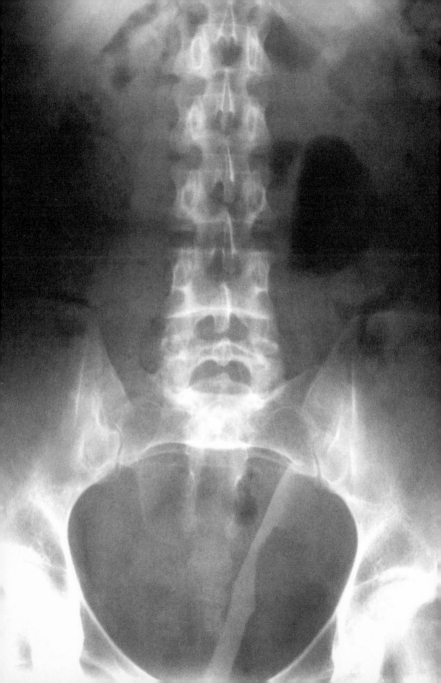

Bad Cavities

You would think that the word "toothbrush" makes it clear that it should be used on the teeth and therefore limited to the oral cavity to prevent cavities. But as you can see, other cavities are targets as well.

Not only would the practice shown here likely make your dentist and most others cringe if they ever found out, but it may also introduce certain bacteria from the oral cavity to the rectal vault. Of course, the issue of toothbrushes retaining bacteria may also come up for those who only use it to clean their teeth. To reduce the likelihood of bacterial retention, the American Dental Association (ADA) recommends washing your toothbrush well after using it and letting it air dry, although not with this kind of air.

Fortunately, the modern toothbrush, introduced in 1938, has nylon bristles, which are less likely to harbor bacteria than the previously used animal-derived bristles (and frankly sound less icky than boar-hair bristles). Nevertheless, it's best to keep your nether regions free of instruments not designed to be used there. So we suggest keeping the toothbrush in the mouth . . . and if you happen to find an "anus brush" and decide to use it, we definitely want to hear about it, and apparently so would a lot of our patients.

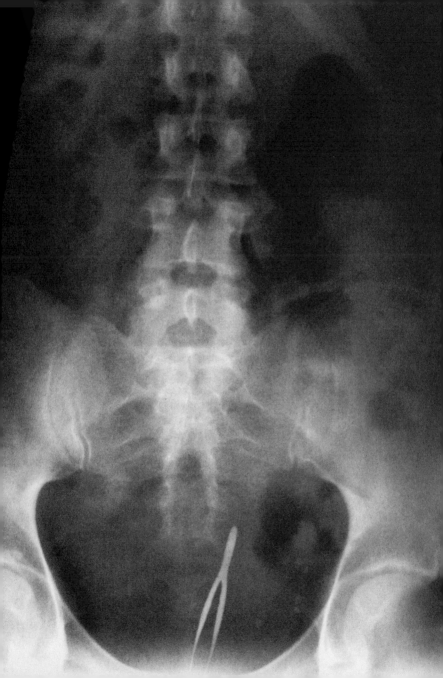

What Hairs Were You Going For?

Ask someone how to remove small items embedded or stuck on the body, such as unwanted hair, thorns, or other small objects, and the answer you will likely get is to use tweezers. However, what do you do when the stuck object is a pair of tweezers itself? Can you tweeze the tweezers?

The patient, a twenty-three-year-old man, presented to the hospital and reported that he had swallowed a pair of tweezers "by mistake" the evening before. The doctors were able to put an endoscope, a tube with a tiny camera at the end, through the mouth and throat to locate and remove the tweezers. Now we wonder what would have happened had the patient swallowed an endoscope.

As a public service, we want to let our readers know that there is a new slang definition of "tweezers" according to the Urban Dictionary . . . and trust us, if you ever need to borrow a tweezer, you really would not want to receive the wrong kind! So what is this new slang meaning? To quote the source, "the act of sticking your arm elbow deep up someone's anus." Hmm, this might give us more material.

REFERENCES

Introduction
Munter D. W. "Rectal Foreign Bodies." www.emedicine.med
scape.com/article/776795-overview. Accessed February 13, 2011.

Not Just for Rice Anymore
Juan S. "Call to abandon wooden chopsticks." http://www.chi
nadaily.com.cn/china/2007-08/10/content_6020039.htm. Accessed February 13, 2011.

Pain in the Glass
T. Lai and P. Aronowitz. "A Meal to Remember." *J Hosp Med* 4,
no.5 (2009): E1–2.

Some Sneezes May Require More Than a "Bless You"
K. Srinivasan. "Black Pepper and Its Pungent Principle—Piperine:
A Review of Diverse Physiological Effects." *Critical Reviews in
Food Science and Nutrition* 47, no.8 (2007): 735–48.

The Pepsi Challange
S. A. Umpierre, J. A. Hill, D. J. Anderson, et al. "Effects of coke
on sperm motility." *The New England Journal of Medicine* 313,
no.21 (1985): 1351.

Message from a Bottle

B. Wansink and C. S. Wansink. "The Largest Last Supper; Depiction of Food Portions and Plate Size Increase Over the Millennium." *International Journal of Obesity* 34 (2010): 943–44.

Don't Want to Be Born with This in Your Mouth

Deeba S., Purkayastha S., Jeyarajah S., et al. "Surgical Removal of a tea spoon from the ascending colon, ten years after ingestion: a case report." http://www.ncbi.nlm.nih.gov/pmc/articles/PMC2769359/. Accessed April 30, 2011.

Mail Foreign Service. "Pictured: The woman who had to go under the knife—after swallowing an entire canteen of cutlery."

Song Y., Guo H., Wu J-Y. "Travel of a mis-swallowed long spoon to the jejunum." *World Journal of Gastroenterology* 15, no.39 (2009): 4984–85.

www.dailymail.co.uk/news/worldnews/article-1223563/The -woman-knife-swallowing-entire-canteen-cutlery.html.Accessed April 30, 2011.

We Thought Tuna Was Good for You

B. Abraham and A. Alao. "An Unusual Foreign Body Ingestion in a Schizophrenic Patient: Case Report." *The International Journal of Psychiatry in Medicine* 35, no.3 (2005): 313–18.

Nemo's Revenge

B. K. P. Goh, Y.-M. Tan, S.-E. Lin, et al. "CT in the Preoperative Diagnosis of Fish Bone Perforation of the Gastrointestinal Tract." *American Journal of Radiology* 187 (2006): 710–14.

Not So Easy to Correct This Mistake
C. S. King, J. E. Smialek, W. A. Troutman. "Sudden Death in Adolescence Resulting from the Inhalation of Typewriter Correction Fluid." *Journal of the American Medical Association* 253(1985): 1604–1606.

Of Cons and Clips
J. E. Losanoff and K. T. Kjossev. "Gastrointestinal 'Crosses': A New Shade from an Old Palette." *Archives of Surgery* 131 (1996): 166–69.

Not So Bright Idea
No author listed. "Information on Compact Fluorescent Lightbulbs (CFLs) and Mercury July 2008." www.cflknowhow.org/cfl-mercury-information.html. Accessed on March 5, 2011.

The Nutty Case of a Nut in a Nutcase
A. H. James and T. J. Allen-Mersh. "Recognition and Management of Patients Who Repeatedly Swallow Foreign Bodies." *Journal of the Royal Society of Medicine* 75 (1982): 107–10.

A Slip *Off* the Tongue
N. E. Tsesmeli, C. G. Savopoulos, A. I. Hatzitolios, et al. "Public Health and Potential Complications of Novel Fashion Accessories: An Unusual Foreign Body in the Upper Gastrointestinal Tract of an Adolescent. *Central European Journal of Public Health* 15, no.4 (2007): 172–74.

The End of Time

E. B. Duboys. "Watch in the Stomach." *Journal of the American Medical Association* 245, no.17 (1981): 1731. M. Bisharat, M. E. O'Donnell, N. Gibson, et al. "Foreign Body Ingestion in Prisoners—The Belfast Experience." *The Ulster Medical Journal* 77, no.2 (2008): 110–14.

Bull's-Eye!

K. De Jongh, D. Dohmen, R. Salgado, et al. "'William Tell' Injury: MDCT of an Arrow Through the Head." *American Journal of Roentgenology* 182 (2004): 1551–53.

Super High or Stupid Guy?

J. Young, D. Beech, and R. Offodile. "Foreign Body Ingestion and Management: 'I Swallowed a Crack Pipe.'" *The American Surgeon* 11 (2007): 1144–46.

See Nothing, Say Nothing, Hear Nothing

D. Dalgorf, K. Trimble, and B. Papsin. "Radiological Features of Ingested Metallic Mesh Earphone Pieces." *Pediatric Radiology* 38 (2008): 1342–44.

It Wasn't Any of Us

A. H. James and T. J. Allen-Marsh. "Recognition and Management of Patients Who Repeatedly Swallow Foreign Bodies." *Journal of the Royal Society of Medicine* 75 (1982): 107–10.

Crossing the Line

D. W. Williams. "Foreign Body in Pharynx." *BMJ* 1 no.4649 (1950): 353. S. T. O'Sullivan, C. M. Reardon, G. T. McGreal, et al.

"Deliberate Ingestion of Foreign Bodies by Institutionalized Psychiatric Hospital Patients and Prison Inmates." *Irish Journal of Medical Science* 165, no.4 (1996): 294–96.

Swallowing Hook, Line, but at Least Not the Sinker
C.-C. Pan, C.-P. Wang, J.-J. Huang, et al. "Intestinal Perforation After the Incidental Ingestion of a Fishhook." *The Journal of Emergency Medicine* 38, no.5 (2010): E45–48.

Something to Fill in the Hole
L. B. Lopez, C. R. Ortega Soler, M. L. de Portela, "[Pica during pregnancy: a frequent underestimated problem]." *Archivos latinoamericos de nutrición* 54, no.1(2004): 17–24.

A Stuck Stick
I. K. Nevins, I. E. Schiek, and A. G. Johnson, "Foreign-body Penetration of the Rectum." *New England Journal of Medicine* 264 (1961): 1127–30.

This Kid Was Hooked
E. Mowed, I. Haddad, and D. J. Gemmel. "Management of Lead Poisoning from Ingested Fishing Sinkers." *Archives of Pediatrics & Adolescent Medicine* 152 (1998): 485–88.

I'm a Barbie Girl, in a Where?
D. Winterman. "What would a real life Barbie look like?" http://news.bbc.co.uk/2/hi/uk_news/magazine/7920962.stm. Accessed February 13, 2011.

If You Have to Put Up Something, This Is Probably the Best Choice

M. Yaman, M. Diefel, C. J. Burul, et al. "Foreign Bodies in the Rectum." *Canadian Journal of Surgery* 36, no.2 (1993): 173–77.

The Best a Man Can Ingest

D. F. Gitlin, J. P. Kaplan, M. P. Rogers, et al. "Foreign-body Ingestion in Patients with Personality Disorders." *Psychosomatics* 28, no.2 (2007): 162–66.

V. Selivanov, G. F. Sheldon, and J. P. Cello. "Management of Foreign Body Ingestion." *Annals of Surgery* 199, no.2 (1984): 187–91.

To Poo or Not to Poo

S. Sathyanarayana, C. J. Karr, P. Lozano, et al. "Baby Care Products: Possible Sources of Infant Phthakte Exposure." *Pediatrics* 121, no.2 (2008): E260–68.

Bad Cavities

No author listed. "Statement on Toothbrush Care: Cleaning, Storage and Replacement." http://www.ada.org/1887.aspx. Accessed on June 12, 2011.

No author listed. "Who invented the toothbrush and when was it invented?" www.loc.gov/rr/scitedr/mysteries/tooth.html. Accessed June, 12, 2011.

What Hairs Were You Going For?

C. P. Kazak, M. Win, and A. Goodman. "Ingestion and Endoscopic Retrieval of Tweezers in a 23-Year-Old Patient." *Southern Medical Journal* 102, no.3 (2009): 338.